Collins

D1102131

gem

Collins
English
Grammar

HarperCollins Publishers
Westerhill Road
Bishopbriggs
Glasgow
G64 2QT
Great Britain

First Edition 1990

First published in this format 2003

Reprint 10 9 8 7 6 5 4

© HarperCollins Publishers 1990

ISBN 978-0-00-722421-0

Collins Gem® is a registered
trademark of HarperCollins
Publishers Limited

www.collinslanguage.com

A catalogue record for this book is
available from the British Library

Prepared for typesetting by the
author

Typeset by Davidson Pre-Press,
Glasgow

Printed and bound in China by
South China Printing Co., Ltd

When you buy a Collins dictionary
or thesaurus and register on
www.collinslanguage.com for the
free online and digital services, you
will not be charged by HarperCollins
for access to Collins free Online
Dictionary content or Collins free
Online Thesaurus content on that
website. However, your operator's
charges for using the internet on
your computer will apply. Costs
vary from operator to operator.
HarperCollins is not responsible
for any charges levied by online
service providers for accessing
Collins free Online Dictionary or
Collins free Online Thesaurus on
www.collinslanguage.com using
these services.

HarperCollins does not warrant
that the functions contained in
www.collinslanguage.com content
will be uninterrupted or error free,
that defects will be corrected, or
that www.collinslanguage.com or
the server that makes it available
are free of viruses or bugs.
HarperCollins is not responsible for
any access difficulties that may be
experienced due to problems with
network, web, online or mobile
phone connections.

Ronald G. Hardie
MA (NZ) MA (Lond.)

EDITOR
Alice Grandison

INTRODUCTION

The *Collins Gem English Grammar* is a compact account of the English language of today. It is intended for those who want to explore how modern English works and to serve the needs of students taking examinations that involve a knowledge of Modern English. In addition, it should prove valuable to anyone who is learning a second language, as it explains grammatical terms that are basic to most languages, such as *adverb, adjective, clause,* and *pronoun*. It also forms a compact reference guide for those learning English as a second language.

The explanations are given in simple and direct language. We start with a general discussion of the main parts of speech. The terms of grammatical description are all defined when they are first used. All the important grammatical and descriptive comments are fully illustrated by tables, lists and, especially, by example sentences on the facing pages. The example sentences are related to the grammatical points by arrowed numbers (→1). The explanations and the examples are designed to work in with each other, while keeping the presentation clear. There are full contents and index sections, so that you can cross-reference points that involve other parts of grammar. Important cross-references are also mentioned in the text.

We have been careful to state when a point of grammar is particularly relevant to spoken or to informal English, or when an expression is more suited to formal speech or writing. We do not attempt to prescribe what a user of English **must** say or write, but sufficient guidance has been provided to allow the reader to make his or her own decisions. What we have to say incorporates what is most representative in current descriptions of the language. It is our belief that *The Collins Gem English Grammar* will prove a valuable resource at any level of study.

R.G.H. 1990

CONTENTS

Parts of Speech

Sentences are made up of **words**. Any number of words can be used in a sentence (→ 1). We can combine words with each other in many ways to make new sentences (→ 2). **Grammar** describes how this is done. Each word in a sentence belongs to a particular set or **class**, depending on how it is used. These classes are called **parts of speech**.

All sentences begin with a capital letter and end in either a full stop, a question mark, or an exclamation mark. When we describe the use of these marks, e.g. commas, semicolons, full stops, brackets, and so on, we are talking about **punctuation**.

The term **clause** is used to describe a group of words that contains a **verb**, the **subject** of that verb, and, often, some other words such as an **object** (→ 3). A sentence can contain one or more **clauses** (→ 4). Many sentences consist of no more than a single clause. Single clause sentences are called **simple** sentences (→ 5).

A clause always contains a **verb** (→ 6). A sentence, however, does not always have to be a clause (→ 7). See p. 228 for more about clauses. A **phrase** is just a **group** of words (→ 8). The term is usually kept for words which go together naturally.

Many words can refer to one thing only or to more than one. We use the terms **singular** and **plural** for this. A more general term is **number**. Pronouns and nouns can be singular or plural in grammatical number. See p. 140.

When we want to identify the speaker or the person spoken about in grammar, we use **first person** to mean the speaker, **second person** to mean the person who is spoken to, and **third person** to mean the person who is spoken about (→ 9). For example, we talk about 'first person plural' or 'third person singular'.

Continued

1 He left us.
  The man in the corner lowered his newspaper.
  Whenever I see Tammy I go quite silly.
  Until tomorrow then.
  Yes.

2 I can help you.   Can I help you?

3 I live in Sussex.   ...where I live.
  Jessica lived in Crowborough at first.
  He was living in Rome that year.
  ...when he had eaten breakfast.

4 I can help you **if you will let me**.
  Whenever you need to talk to someone, just pop in
  and see **if I'm here**.

5 He arrived on Friday.
  My brother loves his skateboard.

6 run   walk
  think   believe

7 Certainly not.   Until tomorrow then.
  Yes.   Why?

8 the other day   my friend Henry
  in spite of   over the hill
  would have been walking

9 Pronouns	*singular*	*plural*
1st person	I	we
2nd person	you	you
3rd person	he, she, it	they
Nouns	the man	the men
	a girl	two girls

Parts of Speech (ctd)

A **verb** informs us about an action or a state of being. Ordinary verbs are called **main verbs** (→ 1). A main verb is sometimes called a 'doing word'. A special group of verbs are called **auxiliary verbs** (→ 2). These combine with main verbs to form different tenses.

A **noun** is a word that labels a thing or an idea (→ 3). Nouns are sometimes called 'naming words'. If we do not want to repeat the same noun in a sentence or a paragraph we can replace it with a **pronoun**. A pronoun is a substitute for a noun phrase or a noun (→ 4).

An **adjective** gives further information about a noun. Adjectives help us describe or pick out which particular thing among many is being referred to (→ 5). Adjectives are sometimes called 'describing words'.

A **determiner** is used to point more precisely to the person, thing, or idea to which reference is being made. Among the determiners are **definite** and **indefinite articles** and **possessives** (→ 6).

An **adverb** gives information about the way that an action is performed or when and where it takes place (→ 7). Some adverbs can also be used to modify adjectives (→ 8), or to introduce a sentence (→ 9). Many adverbs are formed from adjectives by adding *-ly*.

A **preposition** is one of a small group of words that can be used with nouns and verbs. Prepositions give information about position or movement (→ 10). When a preposition is used in front of a noun, the two together do the work of an adverb (→ 11).

A **conjunction** joins two or more nouns or clauses to each other. Conjunctions are sometimes called 'joining words'.

Many words can act as more than one part of speech. It is not unusual for an English word to be a **noun** in one sentence and a **verb** in another sentence (→ 12).

1. come   go   think
   want   economize   believe

2. I **am** thinking.   She **has** seen the film already.
   I **can** help you.   We **might** need to.

3. table   book   ugliness
   time   animal   thing

4. Gary rather liked Sue so **he** asked **her** out.
   The boys were hungry so **they** made tea early.

5. a man   a **tall** man
   their kettle   their **rusty old** kettle
   the cat   the **little tabby** cat

6. **the** cat   **a** man
   my aunt   **their** kettle

7. She ran **quickly** down the path.
   The onlooker chuckled **softly**.
   He lifted the box **gingerly**.

8. A **rather** tall man.   This cake is **quite** nice.
   It was **fairly** good.   It is a **very** hot day.

9. **Certainly**, the harm has been done.
   Honestly, I can't help it.

10. **on** the bridge   **over** the rooftops
    in the morning   **at** the gates

11. He is coming **now**.   He is coming **in the morning**.
    I found him **there**.   I found him **near the gates**.

12. Jamal scored several **runs**.
    She **runs** half a mile each morning.
    I am in the **play** which is on in the village.
    Chris and Doug **play** golf together on Fridays.

Parts of the Sentence

Sentences consist of a number of standard parts, using different parts of speech. The most important parts are:

A. the **subject**, which is either a noun phrase (see p. 120) or a pronoun (see p. 180). Normally the subject comes before the verb phrase in a sentence (→ 1).

B. the **verb phrase**, which includes the main verb and which may have auxiliary verbs to go with it (→ 2). See also pp. 20–65.

C. the **object**, which is a noun phrase or a pronoun (→ 3). Not all verbs need an object. Normally, the object, when there is one, comes after the verb phrase. Some verbs may also need an **indirect object** (→ 4). See also p. 202.

D. an **adverbial**, or **adjunct**, which is an optional part of the sentence.
This may be:
– a single word, an **adverb** (→ 5).
– an **adverbial phrase**, a group of words that functions as an adverb (→ 6).
– an **adverbial clause**, a group of words including a verb, which functions as an adverb (→ 7).

Though some adverbials have a fixed position, most can be added to a sentence in several places: at the beginning, in the verb phrase, or at the end (→ 6). Any number of them can be added, limited only by the sense of the sentence.

E. a **complement**. With certain verbs, such as *be* and *seem,* a complement takes the place of an object.
A complement can be either an adjective or a noun phrase. Complements provide further descriptive detail about the subject (→ 8). See also p. 204.

1 **The girls** had been swimming.
   The new teacher came in.
   They had finished.

2 The girls **had been swimming**.
   The new teacher **came** in.
   They **had finished**.
   She **uses** her sailboard quite a lot.
   Rajiv **was reading** a new novel.
   She **is riding** someone else's horse.

3 She used **her old sailboard**.
   Rajiv was reading **a new novel**.
   Earl found **it**.

4 Hamish gave *me* **a party invitation**.
   Ruth found *Jill* **a nice bunch of flowers**.

5 **Suddenly**, it rained **heavily**.

6 **In the autumn**, it gets very boggy.
   It gets very boggy **in the autumn**.
   It certainly rains **heavily in the autumn**.

7 I'll cut some for you **when I've poured the tea**.
   When I've poured the tea, I'll cut some for you.
   Eric played **while Moira sang**.

8 He became **a new man** with his promotion.
   Andrew is **an apprentice motor-mechanic**.
   He felt **rather silly** when he heard the news.
   They became **good friends** despite the mistake.

Direct and Indirect Objects

The **object** of a sentence (if there is one) normally comes after the verb phrase. Whether there is an object or not depends on the meaning of the verb (→ 1).

For example, if you want to talk about what someone is doing, you might say *'He is writing'* but if you want to talk about what his activity is directed towards, you might say, *'He is writing a book'*.

An object that follows a verb in this manner is called the **direct object** (→ 2). Some verbs also have another sort of object, called an **indirect object**.

An indirect object names the person for or to whom something is done. It is usually needed with verbs like *give, find, owe*. For example, with *give*, we need to name both the thing given and the person to whom it is given (→ 5).

Verbs differ in that some must always take a direct object, some never take a direct object, and others sometimes take one and sometimes don't, depending on the meaning.

When a verb has an object it is called **transitive** (→ 2). When it does not have an object it is called **intransitive** (→ 3). Some verbs may be either **transitive** or **intransitive** (→ 4). When a verb has both an indirect and a direct object it is called **ditransitive** (→ 5).

A direct object is needed where the meaning of the verb requires something to give it a focus. This is why it is sometimes said that a direct object 'complements' a verb.

- Some verbs must have an adverbial as well as a direct object, for example to specify a place (→ 6).

1 She was riding.
   She was riding **her horse**.
   Eric was writing.
   Eric was writing **a letter**.

2 Gerry found **a pen**.
   Our cat doesn't like **milk**.

3 Lynn fainted.
   Patrick screamed.
   Soon, everyone was shouting.

4 Ann was reading (a letter).
   Kim was milking (her goats).

5 Eric owes *Tom* **five pounds**.
   Ron gave *Lyndsey* **a box of chocolates**.
   Susan bought *her rabbit* **some more food**.

6 He placed **the parcel** *on the chair*.
   She put **the umbrella** *in a corner*.

Verbs

Verbs are words that allow us to talk about such things as activities, processes, states of being, and states of mind (→ 1). Verbs divide into two major groups, according to the way they are used in a clause. Those in the larger group are called **main verbs**. The remainder are **auxiliary verbs**.

Verb phrase

A verb can be a single word or a group of associated words (→ 2). When a verb phrase consists of a single word it is called a **simple** verb. Many verbs in English are made by combining an auxiliary verb and a main verb; this is called a **compound** verb.

- When we want to talk about everything to do with a verb, we use the term **verb phrase**.

Main verbs

These are the verbs that we use to indicate actions and states. Most of the verbs in English are main verbs. They are also called **lexical** verbs. Main verbs are divided or **classified** in several ways:
- according to whether they refer to **states** (→ 3) or **actions** (→ 4).
- into **regular** and **irregular** verbs according to the spelling of their forms (→ 5).
- according to whether or not they are followed by an object (→ 6). That is, whether they are **transitive** or **intransitive**. See p. 12.

Auxiliary verbs

These verbs are used in combination with main verbs in order to allow us to talk about different times or periods of time, different degrees of completion, and different amounts of certainty or doubt. There are several types of auxiliary verb. The **primary** auxiliaries help express time, and the **modal** auxiliaries help to express certainty and doubt. See pp. 26–65.

1 This basket **holds** quite a lot.
   John **was reading** Paulette's essay.
   Fiona **is preparing** a talk for next week's class.
   Helen **feels** much happier now.
   I **forgot** that it **was** your birthday.
   Paul **owned** several old motorcycles.

2 he **walks**   he **is walking**
   he **had walked**   he **can walk**
   he **has been walking**
   he **might have been walking**

3 I **can** really **taste** the herbs in this omelette.
   This scarf **belongs** to me.
   I **detest** his brand of intolerant politics.
   She always **liked** stick insects.
   I already **feel** that I **have known** you for ages.

4 Three boys **were kicking** a ball around in the field.
   We **were strolling** across a wide meadow.
   For six hours, Stuart **drove** across open desert.

5 *regular:* talk, talks, talking, talked.
   irregular: swim, swims, swimming, swam, swum.
   irregular: go, goes, going, went, gone.

6 I **can read**.
   We both **read** *the same newspaper*.
   Don't tell *me*.
   We both **ran** away.
   Sue **found** *a bracelet*.
   I **saw** *my best friend* on Friday.

Tense

Verbs enable us to talk about actions and states. They also allow us to talk about the time when the action or state takes place.

- We use the term **tense** to talk about the complete form of the verb phrase and the time scale it expresses.

All main verbs have two **simple** tenses, the **Simple Present** (→ 1) and the **Simple Past** (→ 2). In these tenses the verb is used on its own without any auxiliary verbs.

English verbs also have **compound** tense forms. In these tenses the main verb is accompanied by one or both of the auxiliary verbs *be* and *have*. See p. 76 for more on tenses.

Aspect

The compound tenses of the verb express:
- two **tenses, present** and **past.**
- two **aspects, progressive** and **perfect.**

- We use the term **aspect** to talk about continuing actions (→ 3), (→ 4) versus completed actions or states (→ 5), (→ 6). Simple tenses do not have aspect.

When we add an auxiliary to a main verb to form a compound verb it is because we want to talk about:
- the continuity of an action, by using a form of the auxiliary *be* + *-ing*. This is called the **progressive aspect** (→ 7).
- the completion of an action, by using a form of the auxiliary *have* + a past participle, usually *-ed*. This is called the **perfect aspect** (→ 8).

The two aspects of the verb can be joined so that we can talk about the duration and the completion of an action in the same verb phrase (→ 9).

See pp. 72–74 for more on tense and aspect.

Continued

1 I walk
   she sings
   they come
   you bring

2 I walked
   she sang
   they came
   you brought

3 I am walking
   she is singing
   they are coming
   you are bringing

4 I was walking
   she was singing
   they were coming
   you were bringing

5 I have walked
   she has sung
   they have come
   you have brought

6 I had walked
   she had sung
   they had come
   you had brought

7 I **am** still **studying** French.
   He **was living** in London all that year.
   James **is helping** out with the typing for a week.
   Gloria and Roy **were looking** for a new flat at the
   time.

8 I **have studied** French for four years.
   He **had lived** in London for a year before coming to
   Sussex.
   James **has helped** out before.
   Gloria and Roy **had found** their flat by then.

9 I **have been studying** French for four years.
   I **had been living** in London for four years when I
   met him.
   James **has been helping** us this week.

Tense (ctd)

English verbs are either simple (one word), or compound (several words). Each grouping is called a **tense**. The tenses allow us to refer to different ways of thinking about the time of an action or a state of being.

Simple Tenses

Simple tenses show moments in time, timeless states, and habitual or repetitive actions ($\rightarrow$ 1). The **Simple Present** and the **Simple Past** of regular verbs are formed by using the base form of the verb. See pp. 80–83.

Progressive Tenses

Progressive tenses show duration or continuity ($\rightarrow$ 2). The **Present Progressive** and the **Past Progressive** are formed from either the present or the past tense of the verb *be* + the **present participle** of the main verb. See pp. 84–87.

Perfect Tenses

Perfect tenses show that an action is completed but has some relevance to the present time ($\rightarrow$ 3). The **Present Perfect** and the **Past Perfect** are formed using respectively either the present or past tense of the verb *have* + the **past participle** of the main verb. See pp. 88–93.

Perfect Progressive Tenses

Perfect Progressive tenses show duration, completion, and present relevance ($\rightarrow$ 4). The **Present Perfect Progressive** and the **Past Perfect Progressive** are formed using respectively either the present or past tense of the verb *have* + the **past participle** of *be* + the **present participle** of the main verb. See p. 94.

Other verb forms

Other verb combinations are used for positive or negative statements or to express degrees of time and probability ($\rightarrow$ 5). An important use is to talk about future time ($\rightarrow$ 6).

1 It **tastes** good.
   Julie **keeps** a diary.
   Adrian **kept** a diary once.
   She **hears** voices in the night.
   Rob usually **walks** to school.
   Yesterday he **went** by car.

2 It **is raining** hard this morning.
   It **was raining** at breakfast time yesterday, too.
   She **is eating** a hamburger   *but not It is tasting good.*
   He **was listening** to the radio *but not He was hearing it well.*

3 Ken here **has walked** the Pennine Way.
   He told us he **had attempted** it before but the weather was too wet.
   He **has** never **visited** me.
   She **had missed** the train.

4 I **have been working** hard in the garden all day.
   My mother **has been helping** me.
   Both my sisters **have been working** all day.
   I **had been working** in Italy that summer before going to college.
   Bill, who **had been acting** as an instructor, was promoted to manager.

5 I **like** freshly ground coffee.
   Do you **like** instant coffee?
   I **do** not **like** instant coffee.
   Do you **serve** hot chocolate?
   May I **have** some coffee?

6 You **will be** in Edinburgh before you know it.
   They **will** probably **meet** us at the station.

Types of Main Verb

Verbs of action

Most verbs describe an action such as *walking, running,* or *reading.* When we need a verb to describe a new activity, English grammar allows us to adapt other parts of speech or to invent a new word. Recently adapted or invented verbs include *windsurf* and *gazump* ($\rightarrow$ 1).

- All the tenses can be used with action verbs.

Verbs of state

Some verbs are used to talk about states of being or states of mind ($\rightarrow$ 2).

These include:
- verbs of the senses, e.g. *feel, hear, see, smell, taste*
- verbs of emotion, e.g. *adore, fear, hate, like, love, want, wish*
- verbs of mental activity, e.g. *agree, believe, expect, forget, mean*
- verbs of possession, e.g. *belong, own, possess*

- Verbs of state are not usually used in progressive tenses. When they are used in progressive tenses, they change their meaning ($\rightarrow$ 3).

There are some uses of the verb *be* that allow you to choose between a state or an action meaning. The word used as the complement makes an important difference ($\rightarrow$ 4).

The verb *seem* has a very limited number of adjectives that can be used as its complement ($\rightarrow$ 5).

1   John **is running** for the train.
    Margit **has** just **bought** a new camera.
    She **is putting on** an exhibition of her photographs.
    Russell **has seen** the film already.
    The play **was broadcast** on Radio 3.
    Chris and Debbie **were windsurfing** all afternoon.
    They **were gazumped** by a buyer with more money.

2   I **feel** unhappy.
    I **hate** quarrels.
    These flowers **smell** nice.
    Rob **wishes** he **had not agreed** with the plan.
    We **mean** you no harm.
    That car **belonged** to us once.

3   I'm just **feeling** to see if the bone is broken.
    We **were tasting** some interesting New Zealand
    wines.
    She **is expecting** another child.

4   Bob **is being** silly   ***but not*** Bob is being tall.
    Rupert **is being** nasty   ***but not*** Rupert is being
                                     intelligent.

5   Ron seems **happy**   ***but not*** Ron seems tall.

The Forms of Main Verbs

English verbs have up to five different forms. These are:
1 the base form, e.g. *pull*
2 the 3rd person singular, Simple Present tense, e.g. *pulls*
3 the Simple Past tense, e.g. *pulled*
4 the past participle, e.g. *pulled*
5 the present participle, e.g. *pulling*

- Regular verbs are all formed in the same way, by building on form 1, the **base form**. This is the form you normally find in a dictionary. Most verbs are regular.

- Irregular verbs have different relationships between the other forms and the base form, especially in forms 3 and 4. See p. 24.

Form 1: The **Simple Present** tense has all but one of its forms the same as the base form.

Form 2: When the **Simple Present** tense has a 3rd person singular subject, the verb is formed from the **base form + -s**.

Form 3, the **Simple Past,** and form 4, the **past participle**, are formed from the **base form + -ed.**

Form 5, the **present participle**, is formed from the **base form + -ing.**

A special variation of the base form is the *to infinitive*. There are a number of uses of a verb where both the words *to* + the **base form** must be present.

- The term 'infinitive' is traditional. The base form is sometimes called the 'bare infinitive'.

There are the following exceptions to the rule that the 3rd person singular is formed from the **base form + s** :

Verbs ending in -**o**, -**ch**, -**sh**, -**ss**, -**x**, -**z** or -**zz** add -**es** to make the 3rd person singular, e.g.

torpedo	he torpedo**es**
catch	he catch**es**
focus	he focus**es**
push	he push**es**
miss	he miss**es**
box	he box**es**
buzz	it buzz**es**

Verbs ending in -**y** after a consonant change **y** to **i** and add -**es**, e.g.

carry	he carr**ies**
fly	he fl**ies**
worry	he worr**ies**

Verbs ending in -**y** after a vowel do not change. They only add -**s**, e.g.

say	he say**s**
stay	he stay**s**

There are some exceptions to the rule that the present participle is the **base form** + -***ing***. All verbs that contain a short final vowel in front of a final consonant double the consonant before -***ing***, e.g.

sob	sob**b**ing
bid	bid**d**ing
flog	flog**g**ing
run	run**n**ing
stop	stop**p**ing
get	get**t**ing
put	put**t**ing

Irregular Verbs

Irregular verbs are verbs that do not form the Simple Past tense and the past participle by adding **-ed** to the base form.

The three main groups of irregular verbs

In Group A the base form, the Simple Past and the past participle are the same.

1 the base form   ***put***
2 the Simple Present tense *puts*
3 the Simple Past tense   ***put***
4 the present participle   *putting*
5 the past participle   ***put***

In Group B the Simple Past and the past participle have the same form. Some of these verbs have alternative spellings for the past participle (→ B 2).

1 the base form   ***buy***
2 the Simple Present tense *buys*
3 the Simple Past tense   ***bought***
4 the present participle   *buying*
5 the past participle   ***bought***

In Group C the base form, the Simple Past, and the past participle all have different forms.

1 the base form   ***go***
2 the Simple Present tense *goes*
3 the Simple Past tense   ***went***
4 the present participle   *going*
5 the past participle   ***gone***

A.

bet	cut	let	set	spread
burst	hit	put	shed	thrust
cast	hurt	shut	split	upset

B1.

Base Form	Past Form	Base Form	Past Form
bend	bent	hang	hung
bind	bound	have	had
bleed	bled	hear	heard
bring	brought	keep	kept
build	built	kneel	knelt
buy	bought	lay	laid
catch	caught	make	made
find	found	say	said

B2. The Past form may be either *a* or *b*.

Base Form	Past Form *a*.	*b*.	Base Form	Past Form *a*.	*b*.
burn	burnt	burned	smell	smelt	smelled
dream	dreamt	dreamed	spell	spelt	spelled
lean	leant	leaned	spill	spilt	spilled
learn	learnt	learned	spoil	spoilt	spoiled

C. The Simple Past is like *a*; the Past Participle like *b*.

Base Form	Past Forms *a*.	*b*.	Base Form	Past Forms *a*.	*b*.
arise	arose	arisen	ring	rang	rung
awake	awoke	awoken	rise	rose	risen
bear	bore	borne	saw	sawed	sawn
begin	began	begun	see	saw	seen
bite	bit	bitten	shake	shook	shaken
blow	blew	blown	show	showed	shown
break	broke	broken	shrink	shrank	shrunk
fly	flew	flown	strive	strove	striven
give	gave	given	take	took	taken
know	knew	known	throw	threw	thrown
ride	rode	ridden	write	wrote	written

Auxiliary Verbs

An auxiliary verb is a verb that is used together with a
main verb in order to expand the range of different
meanings that the main verb is capable of expressing,
especially those about time and continuity.

- *be* and *have* are the **primary auxiliaries**. A primary
  auxiliary is used to construct compound tenses.

- *be* is used to make Present and Past Progressive tenses
  ($\rightarrow$ 1) and also for the passive voice ($\rightarrow$ 2). See p. 32 for
  more on *be*.

- *have* is used to make Present and Past Perfect tenses
  ($\rightarrow$ 3). See p. 36 for more on *have*.

- *do* is the **supporting auxiliary**. It is used in forming
  negatives, questions, and emphatic statements in
  clauses which have simple verbs ($\rightarrow$ 4). See p. 40 for
  more on *do*. See pp. 72–79 for more on simple and
  compound verb forms.

- *will, may, might*, and the other verbs listed on
  pp. 44-65 are the **modal auxiliary verbs**, usually
  called simply, **modal verbs**. A modal verb allows us to
  talk about the future as a fact or to talk about future
  actions as possible, doubtful, or necessary ($\rightarrow$ 5).

Auxiliaries can be combined together in a single verb
phrase ($\rightarrow$ 6). For example, a verb phrase may consist of a
modal + a form of *have* + a form of *be* + a **main
verb**.

Continued

1 I **am working**.
Ron **is using** the computer.
We **were** all **asking** about that.
Eric **was teaching** in America in 1985.

2 Suzanne **is liked** by all her friends.
Martin **was sent** to Turkey.

3 Rewi **has finished** fixing the fuse.
George and Alice **have seen** the show already.
Amanda **had** already **eaten** when we arrived.
They **had** not **expected** to see crocodiles.

4 I **do** not **like** mussels at all.
Do you **like** shrimps?
You **do like** shrimps, I hope?

5 Charles **will go** home on Friday.
Charles **may go** home on Friday.
Charles **could go** home on Friday.
Charles **must go** home on Friday.

6 I **could have been making** a bad mistake by trusting him.
Sara **will have lived** in New Zealand for over 2 years now.
You **must have been given** the wrong number.

Auxiliary Verbs (ctd)

The auxiliary verb, or if there is more than one of them,
the first auxiliary verb, performs these grammatical
functions:
- it shows **tense** and is the **finite** part of the verb
  phrase ($\rightarrow$ 1).
- it shows **number** and **person** agreement with the
  subject ($\rightarrow$ 2).
- it will take any **negative** immediately after it ($\rightarrow$ 3).
- it can come before the subject to make a **question** ($\rightarrow$ 4).

Contracted forms

Auxiliaries are very often used in contracted forms. In the
case of *be* and *have,* the contracted form can involve
linking the subject and the auxiliary verb into a single
form e.g. *I'm, I've, we'd, Sue's* (*Sue has* or *Sue is*) ($\rightarrow$ 5).
The contracted negative form, **auxiliary + *n't*,** is common
with all the auxiliaries except *am,* e.g. *hasn't, wouldn't,
don't* ($\rightarrow$ 6).

In British English, the contracted form of ***am not***, when it
is part of a question, is ***aren't I*** ($\rightarrow$ 7).

- Contracted forms are more informal than full forms.
  They are therefore more common in spoken English.
  Full forms are usually preferred in formal written
  English.

Continued

1 I **have** seen it.   She **had** seen it.
   She **has** been thinking   She **had** been thinking.

2 She **has** seen it.   They **have** seen it.
   I **am** looking for it.   You **are** looking for it.

3 I **do not** want to do that.
   She **has not** been thinking.

4 **Do you** want to help us?
   Have you got the correct time?

5 **We're** back!   **We are** back!
   I've found it.   **I have** found it.
   They'd gone when I got there.
   They had gone when I got there.
   Tom's here.   **Tom is** here.

6 She **isn't** (is not) trying.
   We **don't** (do not) live here.
   He **hasn't** (has not) seen it.
   I **can't** (cannot) come.

7 **Aren't I** going to be allowed to come too?
   I'm getting a lift with you, **aren't I**?

Auxiliary Verbs (ctd)

Auxiliaries are used in sentence tags (→ 1). See p. 214 for more about sentence tags.

Auxiliaries are also used to make a short addition to a statement, such as:
– a positive addition to a positive statement, accompanied by *so* or *too* (→ 2).
– a negative addition to a negative statement, accompanied by *neither* or *nor* (→ 3).

• Auxiliaries can be used to give emphasis. When they are emphatic they are never contracted (→ 4).
  In the Simple Present tense and the Simple Past tense the appropriate form of **do** is inserted to show emphasis (→ 5).

• An auxiliary on its own can be used to give a short answer to a question. Whatever auxiliary is used in the question is used on its own in the answer. The main verb is not repeated. Short answers are very common in spoken English (→ 6).

1   You had just bought that carpet, **hadn't you?**
    It's Katie's birthday on Saturday, **isn't it?**
    You are only joking, **aren't you?**

2   I told you I'd find it and **I have too.**
    We thought she was quite sincere and **so she was.**

3   My husband never eats mussels and **neither do** I.
    He doesn't want to speak to Maurice now. – **Nor do** I.
    I can't understand it. – **Neither can** I.

4   You **have** made an ass of yourself!
    Jo **did** well. – Yes, that **was** a nice surprise!
    I **am** fond of Katie. She's so lively.

5   I **do like** Penny. – So do I.
    We **did admire** his clever remarks.

6   **Do** you like avocados? Yes, I **do**. *or* No, I **don't**.
    Have you read anything by Len Deighton? Yes, I **have**.

Be

The verb *be* is used as an auxiliary verb and it can also be used as a main verb. See p. 34.

The verb *be* is irregular. It has eight different forms: *be, am, is, are, was, were, being, been*.
The Simple Present and Simple Past tenses make more changes than those of other verbs ($\rightarrow$ 1), ($\rightarrow$ 2). The present participle is *being* ($\rightarrow$ 4). The past participle is *been* ($\rightarrow$ 5).

* The Simple Present tense forms of *be* are frequently contracted in normal speech. Particularly note the spelling of *they're*, which is the contracted form of *they are* ($\rightarrow$ 3). There are also contractions that apply to the **negative** forms of the verb ($\rightarrow$ 6).

The major uses of *be* as an auxiliary verb are to form progressive compound tenses and the passive voice.

– **Progressive** tenses of main verbs use the appropriate form of *be*, present or past, followed by the present participle. See p. 84 and p. 86.

– The **passive voice** of a main verb uses the appropriate form of *be* followed by the past participle. See p.106.

Any form of *be* is made negative by adding *not* immediately after it ($\rightarrow$ 6). In speech, some forms of *be* also have contracted negative forms.

* Present Tense forms that emphasize the negative:
– *I'm not*;
– *he* / *she* / *it's not*   *you* / *we* / *they're not*;

* Present Tense negative forms used less emphatically:
– *he* / *she* / *it isn't*;   *you* / *we* / *they aren't*

* Past Tense negative forms used less emphatically:
– *he* / *she* / *it wasn't*;   *you* / *we* / *they weren't*

Continued

1 I **am** late.   We **are** late.
   You **are** late.   You **are** late.
   He **is** late.   They **are** late.

2 I **was** late.   We **were** late.
   You **were** late.   You **were** late.
   She **was** late.   They **were** late.

3 **I'm** here.   **We're** here.
   You're here.   **You're** here.
   He's here.   **They're** here.

4 He is **being** very helpful these days.

5 We have **been** ready for an hour.

6 **I'm not** late, am I?   You **aren't** late.
   You're not late.   He **isn't** late.
   He's not late.   We **aren't** late.
   We're not late.   They **aren't** late.
   They're not late.

   I **wasn't** late.
   You **weren't** late.
   He **wasn't** late.
   We **weren't** late.
   They **weren't** late.

Be (ctd)

The verb *be* is also used as a main verb. It is commonly found joining a subject to its complement.

The **main verb** use of *be* is to talk about:
- feelings and states. For this we use the simple tenses of the verb with a suitable adjective ($\rightarrow$ 1). See p. 80.
- people's behaviour. For this we use the progressive tenses of the verb with a suitable adjective ($\rightarrow$ 2). See p. 84.

- *be* + the *to infinitive* is sometimes used to refer to future time ($\rightarrow$ 3). This is a rather formal use, which often appears in news reports. See pp. 96–105.

- *It* + *be*: we use *it* as a dummy subject for a noun phrase such as one that refers to time ($\rightarrow$ 4), distance ($\rightarrow$ 5), weather ($\rightarrow$ 6), or cost ($\rightarrow$ 7). In this use, *be* is always singular.

- *There* + *is / are* is used to talk about the existence of something. In this use, the form that *be* takes may be singular or plural, depending on the number of the noun, and *be* is sometimes contracted ($\rightarrow$ 8).

To make the progressive tenses of the main verb *be* we have to use *be* twice, once as an auxiliary and once as a main verb ($\rightarrow$ 9).

The question form of clauses with the verb *be* in them is made by putting the appropriate form of *be* right in front of the subject ($\rightarrow$ 10).

1 I **am delighted** with the news but he **is not happy**.
   She **was busy** so she **was not able** to see me.

2 I **am not being** slow, I **am being** careful.
   You **were being** very rude.

3 The Prime Minister **is to visit** Hungary in October.
   The Archbishop **is to have** talks with the Pope next
   month.

4 Hurry up, **it's eight thirty**!
   Is it? I didn't know **it was so late**.

5 **It is** thirty miles to Glasgow.
   Come and visit us. **It's not very far**.

6 **It is cold** today but **it isn't wet**.

7 **It is very expensive** to travel by air.

8 **There's** a spare sail in the locker.
   There was a stiff breeze blowing.
   There isn't enough petrol for the journey.
   There's a petrol station on the way, **isn't there**?

9 You **are being** most annoying!
   I know I **am being** silly, but I am frightened.

10 **Are you** better now?
   Is he free this morning?
   Was he cooking supper?

Have

The verb *have* is used as an auxiliary verb (→ 1) and also as a main verb (→ 2). See p. 38.

The verb *have* has the forms: *have, has, having, had*. The base form of the verb is *have*. The present participle is *having*. The Past tense and past participle form is *had*.

- The present and past forms are frequently contracted in everyday speech, especially when *have* is being used as an auxiliary verb (→ 3).
  Caution: The form *have* contracts to *'ve*. Especially after other auxiliary verbs (→ 4), this can sound rather like *of*. Avoid the common mistake of writing *of* in this case.

As an **auxiliary** verb *have* is used to make the **Perfect tenses** of main verbs.
- The **Perfect** tenses of main verbs use the appropriate form of *have*, present or past, followed by the past participle (→ 5). See p. 88 and p. 90.

The negative of a clause containing a compound verb with *have* is made by adding *not* or another negative word immediately after the appropriate form of *have* (→ 6). In speech, some forms of *have* also have contracted negative forms.

- Present tense and Past tense forms that emphasize the negative element (→ 7):
  I / we / you / they've not; *he / she / it's not*
  I / we / you / he / she / it /they'd not

- Present tense and Past tense negative forms that are used less emphatically (→ 8):
  I / we / you / they haven't; *he / she / it hasn't*
  I / we / you / he / she / it /they hadn't

Continued

1 She **has run** herself a luxurious, deep, bubble bath.
   Katie **had read** about the concert in the newspaper.

2 She is **having** a bath at the moment.
   The driver has **had** his breakfast, so we can go.

3 The contracted forms are:
   have = 've   I**'ve** seen the Queen.
   has = 's   He**'s** gone on holiday.
                            Ian**'s** behaved badly.
   had = 'd   You**'d** best be gone.
                            Tracey**'d** left them behind.

4 She **would've** given you a warm welcome.
   You **could've** stayed the night with us.
   If he**'d 've** asked, I **might've** lent him my car.

5 I **have seen** several possible sites for the house.
   I **had seen** several sites for the new house.

6 You **have never seen** such luxury.
   Rachel **had never seen** such luxury.
   She **had barely arrived** when Paul turned up.

7 She**'s not** told me about it yet.
   We**'ve not** been here before.
   They**'d not** seen him for weeks.

8 He **hasn't** found anywhere to stay this holiday.
   We **haven't** been here before.
   They **hadn't** looked very hard, I feel.

Have (ctd)

The **main verb** use of *have* is to talk about:

A. states or conditions, such as possession or relationship.

– In these uses, progressive tenses are not possible.
   With this meaning *have* can be used alone, adding only
   not to make negatives and adding nothing to make
   questions (→ 1). It can also be used with forms of *do* to
   make negatives and questions, especially in American
   English (→ 2).

• *have got* is an informal form of this main verb use of
   have, often used in speaking, especially in British
   English (→ 3).

B. activities (→ 4), including those such as eating (→ 5),
and leisure (→ 6).

– With this meaning of *have,* negatives and questions are
   formed using one of the forms of *do* (→ 5), (→ 6).

– Contractions and weak forms are not possible with this
   meaning.

• *have got* (in the sense of *possess*) is not used with this
   meaning.

C. to express obligation using *have to* or *have got to* (→ 7).

– With these meanings progressive tenses are possible (→ 8).

• When *have* is a main verb, it makes Perfect forms like
   all other main verbs. This means that it is possible to
   use *have* twice in Present or Past Perfect sentences,
   once as an auxiliary verb and once as a main verb
   (→ 9).

1   **I have** something for you.
    We haven't anything for you today.
    Have you no sense of shame?
    The driver **has had** his breakfast, so we can go.
    We **had** a good time.

2   **Do you have** a pen?
    Does she have my umbrella?
    She doesn't have any.
    Do you have time to see me now?

3   **I haven't got** any brothers or sisters.
    Has she got my umbrella? – Yes, she has.
    She hasn't got any.
    I hadn't got enough money for the bus.

4   **He was having** a shower when I phoned.

5   I'm **having** lunch at twelve o'clock.
    Come and **have** a sandwich with me,
    No thanks. I **don't** usually **have** lunch.

6   He's **having** a day off.
    Did you **have** a good holiday?

7   **I've got to** go now, I'm afraid.
    Do you have to leave so soon?
    Have you got to leave so soon?

8   I am **having to** spend less on records.

9   We **have had** enough, thank you.
    They **had had** quite a number of warnings.

Do

The verb **do** is used as an auxiliary verb (→ 1), (→ 2).
It can also be used as a main verb. See p. 42. When **do** is
used as an auxiliary verb it is a **supporting verb**.
Because a main verb cannot combine directly with negatives or
make questions, **do** is used to support the main verb (→ 4).
It is also used to stand in for another verb to avoid repetition
as in examples 6 to 10.

The verb **do** is irregular. It has five different forms:
do, does, doing, did, done.
The base form of the verb is **do**. The Simple Past form,
did, is the same throughout. The present participle is
doing. The past participle is **done**.

The Simple Present tense and the Simple Past tense can
be used as an auxiliary verb (→ 1), (→ 2). The participial
forms are not used as part of the auxiliary verb. As an
auxiliary, **do** is not used with **modal** verbs.

As an **auxiliary** verb **do** is used in these ways:
– to help make the negative and question forms of
  Simple Present and Simple Past Tenses (→ 3).
– to make the negative form of a command (→ 4).
– to make a command more persuasive (→ 5). See p. 218
– to avoid repeating a main verb in the following situations:
  additions (→ 6), commands (→ 7), sentence tags (→ 8),
  short answers (→ 9).
– in comparisons (→ 10).

The positive forms of **do** cannot be contracted. In speech,
the negative has contracted forms (→ 11).

• Present Tense negative forms:
  I / we / you / they **don't;** he / she / it **doesn't**
  Past Tense negative form:
  I / we / you / he / she / it / they **didn't**

Continued

1 I **do** not want it.   We **do** not want it.
  You **do** not want it.   You **do** not want it.
  He **does** not want it. They **do** not want it.

2 I **did** not want it.   We **did** not want it.
  You **did** not want it.   You **did** not want it.
  She **did** not want it. They **did** not want it.

3 Oh dear, I **didn't feed** the alligator this morning.
  Do you **know** what time it is?
  Did Tim **pay** for his ticket last night?

4 **Don't** talk!
  Don't run!

5 **Do** let me see it!

6 They often go to the cinema, **and so do** we.

7 Don't run on the road! Don't **do** it, I tell you!

8 You live in Glasgow, **don't** you?

9 Do you play cricket? – No, I **don't**.
  Did they tell you the news? – Yes, they **did**.
  Jim likes music, I think. Yes, **he does**.

10 She **sings** better than I **do**.

11 I **don't** (do not) agree with you.
   She **doesn't** (does not) live here now.
   They **didn't** (did not) buy any coffee.

Do (ctd)

When *do* is a main verb, it has a range of meanings that includes *carry out, perform, fix,* or *provide*. It is sometimes used in place of a more specific verb (→ 1). It is then used with the full range of tenses and forms (→ 2). See also p. 40.

- The main verb use of *do* can be used to talk about:
  – habits (→ 3).
  – behaviour (→ 4).
  – plans (→ 5).

As a main verb, *do* makes negatives and questions like all other main verbs:
  – in the Simple Present tense with auxiliary *do* (→ 6).
  – in the Simple Past tense with auxiliary *did* (→ 7).

This means that it is possible to use *do* twice in negative and interrogative sentences; once as an auxiliary verb and once as a main verb.

• As a main verb, *do* can be used with modal verbs (→ 8).

1 I'll **do** the lawn now.   I'll **mow** the lawn now.
   I'll **do** you.   I'll **punch** you.
   We don't **do** coach parties.
   We don't **serve** coach parties.

2 **Are** you **doing** your homework?
   You **have been doing** well this term.
   She **had done** enough, so she stopped.
   This **has been done** before.

3 I **do** the washing up every evening.
   This what I usually **do**.

4 He **did** something rather foolish.
   I **don't do** the ironing very often.
   What **have** you **been doing** all day?

5 What **are** you **doing** on Sunday?

6 What **does** he **do** for a living?
   Do I **do** it this way?
   No, you **don't do** it like that at all.

7 **Did** Henry **do** it, then?
   Didn't Henry **do** it, then?
   He **didn't do** it, you know.

8 They **will do** it for you, if you ask nicely.
   I **can do** it, but I **shouldn't do** it.

Modal Verbs

Modal verbs are particular kinds of **auxiliaries** (→ 1).

Modal verbs are used when you need to add special elements of meaning to a main verb, e.g.:
- to express different degrees of doubt and possibility about the action of the main verb (→ 2).
- to express degrees of future possibility, ranging from the definite future, *will*, to the possible future, *may*, and the conditional future, *could* (→ 3).
- to request or give permission for an action to take place (→ 4).
- to make a prohibition, when used with a negative (→ 5).
- to make an assumption (→ 6).
- to express obligation and duty (→ 7).
- to refer to characteristic behaviour (→ 8).
- to add politeness to a request which might otherwise sound abrupt (→ 9).
- to make conditional sentences (see p. 240).
- in reported speech (see p. 246).

All the modals can refer to a time range that reaches from the immediate present to some future time, so that they can all be used for future reference, especially when they are used with a time adverbial (→ 3). See p. 50–64.

- Some modals can refer to a time range that goes back from the immediate present to some indefinite past time. They can refer to habitual action when they are used with a time adverbial (→ 10).

Continued

1 Look, I **can** ride it! – So you **can**.
Might I use your telephone? – Of course you **may**.
Do you think that she **will** come? – I'm sure she **will**.
I **must** get our tickets today.

2 I **may** not **be able** to do it.
I think that I **might have caught** your cold.
I **could ask** on your behalf, if you like.
You **couldn't do** it yourself, **could** you?

3 You **will be seeing** her **on Friday** at Jean's place.
I **may** be late home **tomorrow evening**.
I **could bring** some more bread home with me
tonight.

4 **May** I come in? – Yes, you **may**.
You **can** borrow my car tonight.

5 You **shouldn't** use this copier without permission.
You **cannot** borrow my car tonight.
He **must not** see this letter.

6 The weather's so bad the flight **could** be late.
It **might** be all over by the time we get there.
He **may** be very cross about the whole business.

7 I **must** give in my essay today.
Helen **ought to** tell the truth.

8 She **can** be very charming on these occasions.

9 **Would you** please close the door.

10 When I was young, I **would** ride my bike round and
round the lawn.

Modal verbs (ctd)

Form

Unlike other verbs, modal verbs have only one form, the
base form, and only one tense, the Simple Present ($\rightarrow$ 1).
They do not have a *to* infinitive.
They have no –s inflection in the 3rd person singular ($\rightarrow$ 2).

- Since modal verbs do not have past tense forms you
  have to use other verbs to provide some of the modal
  meanings in the past, e.g. past necessity is expressed
  by *had to* instead of *must* ($\rightarrow$ 3).

- The modals **shall** and **will** are usually contracted to *'ll*
  in spoken English. All the negative forms can be
  contracted to form a single word such as *can't, won't,
  wouldn't*. These contracted forms are common in both
  spoken and written English ($\rightarrow$ 4). There are other
  contracted forms such as *he'll, we'll, shan't,* and
  they'll, which are common in spoken English but rare
  in written English.

- Several verbs act as modals sometimes and as full main
  verbs at other times ($\rightarrow$ 5). These are called
  semi–modal verbs.

Position

Modals come before any other auxiliary verb or main verb
in the verb phrase. As they come first in the verb phrase,
they are always finite.

- Modal verbs are followed by the **base form** of the verb
  if there is no other auxiliary verb present ($\rightarrow$ 6).
  If one of the auxiliary verbs *have* or *be* follows the
  modal verb, the main verb will take the appropriate
  present or past participle form ($\rightarrow$ 7).

- In negative sentences *not* comes immediately after the
  modal verb and in front of all the other verbs ($\rightarrow$ 8).

- *can* cannot be combined with the auxiliary form *have,* but
  the negative form *can't* can be so combined ($\rightarrow$ 9).

1 You **will** be seeing her **on Friday** at Jean's place.
   I **may** be late home **tomorrow evening.**
   I **might** go to visit Grandma **on Saturday**.

2 **He will** be seeing her on Friday.
   She may be late home.

3 I **must** visit Auntie May.
   I **had to** visit Auntie May.

4 I will / shall = **I'll**   We will / shall = **we'll**
   You **mustn't** use my comb, Jane.
   John **can't** come to my party; I don't want him.

5 How **dare** he!
   He **dares** to ask me to do his washing!
   She **need** not come if that is how she feels.
   Monica **needs** a new raincoat.

6 Yes, you **may borrow** those earrings tonight.
   You **can go** at 8 p.m. It's too early to go now.
   People **must think** about the consequences of their
   actions.

7 I **may have offended** him.
   You **could have looked** for it yourself.
   Janice **might be coming** too.
   Sian **will have been worried** about her, I'm sure.

8 The train may be late. Anna **may not wait** for it.
   They **might not wait** for you after 9 o'clock.

9 They **can't have seen** him.   *but not* They can have
                                       seen him.

Can and Could

Both these verbs indicate ability in some respect. The use of *could* is usual in clauses that contain a reference to past time ($\rightarrow$ 1), ($\rightarrow$ 2).

Can and *could* are used:
- to indicate that you know how to do something ($\rightarrow$ 1).
- to show ability to do something ($\rightarrow$ 2). (Compared with *be able to,* *can* indicates ability of a more general nature that includes 'is permitted to'.)
- to make polite requests or to ask for permission: *could* is more tentative than *can* ($\rightarrow$ 3). (This use of *can* is not ungrammatical, but it blurs the distinction between ability and possibility in requests: *may* is more formal.)
- to express the possibility of an action in the future, especially when the possibility is related to plans or projects ($\rightarrow$ 4). (Compare with *may*, where the possibility referred to is still uncertain and in the future.)
- to express the possibility of an action in the present ($\rightarrow$ 5).
- to talk about actions that were possible but did not happen, using *could* + the Perfect form of *have* ($\rightarrow$ 6).
- using the Perfect form of *have*, to speculate about actions that have recently taken place ($\rightarrow$ 7).

A distinction between *can* and *could* is observed in conditionals. *Could* is used when the conditions are not met ($\rightarrow$ 8).

When changing sentences from direct to reported speech *can* is usually changed to *could* ($\rightarrow$ 9).

can
Negative form :   *cannot* ($\rightarrow$ 10).
Contracted negative form: *can't* ($\rightarrow$ 11).

could
Contracted negative form: *couldn't* ($\rightarrow$ 12).

1 Morag **can** speak French quite well now.
I **can** play chess now but I **couldn't** play it two years ago.

2 When I was younger I **could** play tennis really well.
Winston is so strong he **can** lift me right off my feet.
Winston **is able to** lift weights of over 100kg.
Winston **can** lift me off my feet whenever he likes!

3 **Can** I borrow the car tomorrow evening, Mum?
May I take the computer home to finish the project?
Could I come with you on the trip?

4 We **can** go to Paris next week since you are free.
We **could** go to Paris next week if you are free.
We **may** go to Paris but it depends on our finances.

5 You **can** swim off these rocks; it is quite safe there.
We **could** swim off the rocks if we take care.

6 Mary **could have stopped** the quarrel but she didn't.

7 Who **could / can have broken** the window?
Who **could have guessed** that he would come?

8 **If** Louisa is coming, she **can** look after the children for a while.
If Helen had more money, she **could** buy a computer.

9 Bernard said, "I **can** do it for you, Sue."
Bernard said that he **could** do it for Sue.

10 I **cannot** understand why he did it.

11 I **can't** help it. Give me a hand, **can't** you.

12 I **couldn't** help it.

May and Might

Both *may* and *might* are used in requests and in expressions of possibility for the present and future (→ 2), (→ 4), (→ 8).

May and *might* are used as follows:
- *may* is used to ask permission in a more formal way than *can* (→ 1). *Might* is also sometimes used to ask permission, especially when you want to show that you are uncertain about the response (→ 2).
- *may* is used to give permission, particularly when applied to *you, he, she, they* or a proper noun, to show that the speaker is allowing something to happen (→ 3).
- to express the possibility of some future action; *might* is more tentative than *may* (→ 4).
- *may* is often used for politeness, to make an order appear as a request; *might* is used to make the speaker more remote from the request. Because of this it can seem very formal (→ 5).
- *might* is used when someone is trying to persuade another person to do something, perhaps with some degree of irritation (→ 6), but it can also be used for a casual request (→ 7).
- When *might* is used in a conditional sentence, the *if* clause can be in the present or the past tense. Compare with *could* (→ 8). See p. 48.

When changing sentences from direct to reported speech *may* is usually rewritten as *might* (→ 9).

may
Contracted negative form: none or *mayn't* (rare).

might
Contracted negative form: *mightn't* (→ 10).

1 **May** I have a drink, please?
   May I use your ruler? I've lost mine.

2 **Might** I bring my cousin when we come to dinner?

3 You **may** go, Paul, but I won't allow Peter to go.
   Louisa said, "Martin **may** go because he has tidied his room."
   Jan **may** have a chocolate since she has finished first.

4 The weather **may / might** be better tomorrow.
   Craig **may / might** know his results soon.
   We **may / might** go to the cinema tonight.

5 **May** I have a word with you?
   Might I have a word with you?

6 You **might** give me some cake too, Lucy.
   Anna, you **might** tell me what he said. I want to know.

7 If you're going out, **might** I ask you to post my letter?

8 If Louisa **comes**, she **might** look after the children.
   If Louisa **came**, she **might** look after the children.

9 "**May** I come with you?" Norma asked.
   Norma asked if she **might** come with them.

10 He **mightn't** have enough money.
    You might be lucky, **mightn't** you?

Must

Must is used to express obligation, compulsion and accepted truths. It can only be used for present and future reference. When the past is involved, you use *have to*.

Must is used:
- to express obligation ($\rightarrow$ 1).
- to give orders firmly and positively ($\rightarrow$ 2).
- to give advice or make recommendations emphatically ($\rightarrow$ 3).
- to express a positive assumption that the speaker is making about the truth of something ($\rightarrow$ 4). When this sort of statement is made in the negative or interrogative, *can* is used instead ($\rightarrow$ 5).

• *must* can be used in the interrogative, but many speakers prefer *have to* instead ($\rightarrow$ 6).

You can use *must* with a negative:
- to give a definite prohibition ($\rightarrow$ 7)
- to talk about an event or state that is unacceptable. ($\rightarrow$ 8).

• Note that to express the fact that you are not obliged to do something, you use *do not have to* ($\rightarrow$ 9).

• It is necessary to change *must* to *have to* when changing sentences from direct to reported speech. ($\rightarrow$ 10).

must
Contracted negative form: *mustn't* ($\rightarrow$ 11).

1 All pupils **must** do an hour's homework each evening.

2 You **must** go and visit your grandmother today.
   You **must** all do your homework.

3 You **must** get one of these new mixers – they're great!
   You really **must** read *Out of Africa* – it's very good.

4 You **must** be mad! Mary **must** be joking about him!
   There **must** be a mistake: there is something missing.
   Shah is here. It **must** be Tuesday.

5 **Can** Mary be joking? **Can** she really mean that?
   You **can't** be serious!
   It **can't** be true!

6 **Must she** go alone?
   Must I invite Helen?
   Does she have to go alone?
   Do I have to invite Helen?

7 You **must not** cross the junction when the light is red.
   You **must not** throw your litter on the grass.

8 There **mustn't** be a mistake.
   The whale **must not** become extinct.

9 Compare:
   You **must not** waste your time visiting her.
   You **don't have to** waste your time visiting her.

10 "I **must** visit Sara in hospital this evening," said Ian.
    Ian said that he **had to** visit Sara in hospital.

11 You **mustn't** ever do that again.

Shall and Will

The modal verb **will** followed by the **base form** of a main verb is the normal way to express simple future time reference in English.

- Older grammar books used to say that *I* and *we* must always be used with **shall**. The use of **will** was reserved for *you, he, she, it*, and *they*. Some writers still make this distinction, but there is no really good reason for it. The modal verb **shall** is not used very much in modern English, except in questions ($\rightarrow$ 1).
  Any distinction between **will** and **shall** is difficult to make in spoken English, since the contracted form, *'ll*, is used to mean both **shall** and **will**.

shall is used:
- with questions involving *I* and *we* when the speaker is making a suggestion ($\rightarrow$ 1).
- with *I* and *we* to show intentions and to make promises ($\rightarrow$ 2).
- with *you, he, she, it*, and *they*, to show willingness ($\rightarrow$ 3).
- to show insistence. Full forms are normally used, and are stressed in speech ($\rightarrow$ 4).

will is used:
- everywhere that **shall** can be used, except for questions with *I* or *we*.
- to make polite requests and to give invitations ($\rightarrow$ 5).
- to give orders ($\rightarrow$ 6).
- to show persistence (full form with stress) ($\rightarrow$ 7).
- to show prediction ($\rightarrow$ 8).

will
Contracted form: *'ll* ($\rightarrow$ 9).
Contracted negative form: *won't* ($\rightarrow$ 10).

shall
Contracted form: *'ll*
Contracted negative form: *shan't* (used mainly in British English) ($\rightarrow$ 11).

1 **Shall** I help you? **Shall** I cook supper?
   Shall we go to the cinema tonight?

2 Don't worry. I **shan't / won't** be late and Helen **won't**
   be late either.
   We **shall / will** be in touch.
   I **shall / will** try to ensure that you get a good room.

3 You **shall** have the run of the house.
   He **shall** be well treated.
   You **shall** have your money next week.

4 You **shall** do what I tell you, so there!
   Jane **shall** go to Mary's even if I have to carry her
   there.
   I **shall / will** make a fuss and you can't stop me.

5 **Will** you help me look for my purse?
   Will you come to supper on Friday?

6 You **will** finish your work before you watch TV, **won't**
   you?
   Louisa, **will** you please be quiet!

7 Peter **will** fight with Paul, whatever I do.
   No wonder you feel sick. You **will** eat chocolate all day
   long.

8 The match **will** be finished by now.
   Louisa **will** have reached home by now.

9 He**'ll** be home soon.

10 Eve **won't** speak to Harriet.

11 Don't worry, we **shan't** be late.

Should

The modal verb *should* is used in the following ways:
- to indicate moral obligation ($\to$ 1). Compare *ought to* on p. 60.
- to give advice or instructions ($\to$ 2).
- to suggest that something follows on logically from what has just been said ($\to$ 3).
- in a conditional clause, *should* can be used to show politeness. This use is usual in formal written communication ($\to$ 4).

- After certain set expressions such as, *it is a pity that, it is odd that, I am sorry / surprised that*, *should* can be used with the main verb ($\to$ 5). This is a more formal use than the same expression without *should*.

- *should* + the perfect form of *have* can be used to express regret or annoyance about something that was done or not done ($\to$ 6). Compare with *ought to*.

- When changing sentences from direct to reported speech *should* usually replaces *shall* after the first person singular or plural (*I , we*) ($\to$ 7). Historically, *should* was the past tense of *shall*.

Should can be used with *I* or *we* to refer to some possible future event or circumstance which seems desirable but will happen only if other conditions are right. This form is usually found together with an *if* clause. If there is not an *if* clause, it is understood to mean '*if conditions are right*' ($\to$ 8). In this sense, *would* is more common in modern spoken English ($\to$ 9).

1 They **should** do what John suggested.
   People **should** report vandals to the police.
   John recommended that the car **should** be abandoned.
   Mary insisted new clothes **should** be bought for Jane.

2 You **should** undo the top screws first and then lift the
   door off.
   You **should** keep your credit card separately from your
   chequebook.

3 They left here at 6 o'clock; they **should** be home now.

4 If you **should** decide to go, please contact us.
   Should you need more information, call the manager.

5 It's a pity that Jane **should** remain so angry.
   I am surprised that you **should** care.

6 He **should have stopped** at the red light.
   You **should have told** me you were ill.

7 Anna said that I **should** go to Lisbon next week.

8 I **should** love to visit Peru **if I had the money.**
   I **should** love to visit Barbados.
   I **should** be very cross **if they didn't give me a cer-
   tificate**.
   We **should** hate to miss seeing the play
   (but something could interfere with our plans).

9 I **would** love to visit Peru.
   I **would** be very cross if they didn't give me a certifi-
   cate.
   I **would** hate to miss seeing the play.

Would

The modal verb **would** is commonly used as follows:
– to signal a polite request (→ 1).
– to offer something politely (→ 2).
– together with *like* as a polite form of *want* (→ 3).
– to refer to characteristic activity, with the meaning of *used to* (→ 4).
– to show persistence in an activity (→ 5): **would** is sometimes stressed here. It can also be used to answer a complaint when the speaker feels that someone has brought about his or her own misfortune.
– to express and ask about probability (→ 6).
– to suggest what the speaker believes would take place in a certain set of circumstances, usually with an **if** clause (→ 7).

When changing sentences from direct speech to reported speech, **will** is usually changed to **would** (→ 8). Historically, **would** was the past tense of **will**.

would

Contracted form:	**'d** (→ 9).
Contracted negative form:	**wouldn't** (→ 10).

1 **Would** you mind moving your bag?
 Would you lend me your bicycle, please?

2 **Would** you **like** some tea or coffee?

3 We **would like** to see Mr Brown now, please.
 My friends **would like** to see your garden.

4 Jeff **would** eat chocolate all day – no wonder he got fat.
 Liz **would** exercise until she dropped.

5 John **would** keep naging at her, though I asked him not to.
 Well, you **would** keep doing it. I warned you.
 I wish they **wouldn't** keep asking me to visit them.

6 I saw a girl at the window. Who **would** that be?
 Oh, that **would** be his elder sister!

7 I **would** have taken it if it had been offered to me.
 I **wouldn't** refuse if you asked me to have some more.
 Brian **would** have phoned the police if it had been his car.

8 Anna said, "Raymond **will** help you next week."
 Anna said that Raymond **would** help us the following week.
 James said, "The car **won't** start!"
 James said that the car **wouldn't** start.

9 **I'd** have done it too, given the chance.
 We'd like to look at the garden.
 He'd have been very angry if he had known about it.

10 Even if he'd known about it, he **wouldn't** have been angry.

Ought to

The verb *ought to* does not have a past form. It is only used with reference to the present and the future.

In negatives *not* comes between *ought* and *to* (→ 1). In questions the subject comes between *ought* and *to* (→ 2). In short answers, the use of *to* is optional (→ 3).

ought to is used as follows:
– to express an obligation or an expectation that someone should do something (→ 4).
– to express the likelihood of something happening (→ 5).
– **ought to + have + past participle of main verb** is used to express regret that something was not done or to reproach someone for doing or not doing something (→ 6).

The use of *ought to* is less strong than *should* or *must* (→ 7). The distinctions are as follows:
– to give general advice, use *ought to*.
– when you want to add a reproach, use *should*.
– if you want to be insistent or suggest a threat, use *must*.

• In questions *should* is frequently used instead of *ought to* because it sounds more natural (→ 8).

ought to

Contracted negative form: *oughtn't (to)* (→ 2), (→ 3).

1 You **ought to** listen carefully.
   You **ought not to** tease your sister like that.

2 **Ought** you **to** do that? I don't think you ought to.
   Oughtn't Jane **to** leave for home now? It's late.

3 **Oughtn't** Helen **to** go now? – Yes, she **ought (to)**.
   Lucy **ought to** apologize to me. – No, she **oughtn't (to)**.

4 They knew they **ought to** leave promptly.
   Lucy **ought to** go today and Helen **ought to** go later.
   People **ought to** give more money to famine relief.
   Children **ought to** clean their teeth regularly.

5 Annabel **ought to** be here by now.
   They **ought to** finish cooking the lunch soon.
   My exam results **ought to** be announced on Friday.

6 I **ought to have spoken up** earlier. I am sorry I
   didn't.
   You **ought to have offered** to help.
   We **ought to have given** more money to famine relief.

7 Compare:
   You **ought to** consider the feelings of others.
   You really **should** be more considerate in future.
   You **must** not go around upsetting people like that!
   You **must tell** the police if you think someone is doing
   something illegal.

8 **Ought** I **to** report it to someone in authority?
   Should I report it to someone in authority?

Dare and Need

Two verbs, ***dare*** and ***need***, have characteristics of both modal verbs and main verbs. Because of this, they are called **semi-modals**. They sometimes behave like modal verbs and do not add *-s* to the form that goes with *he, she*, and *it*. That is, they have no third person singular inflection. They are then followed by the **base form** of a main verb ($\rightarrow$ 1).

- ***dare*** has a past form, although this is rather rare as a modal. The past of ***need (needed)*** is not used as a modal ($\rightarrow$ 2).

The modal uses of these verbs are all **negatives** or clauses in the **interrogative** mood. ***Dare*** and ***need*** sometimes behave like main verbs with *-s* inflection. In this case they are followed by the ***to*** infinitive. They can also use the auxiliary ***do*** and have the whole range of tenses appropriate to a main verb ($\rightarrow$ 3).

When ***dare*** or ***need*** is used as a modal verb in a **statement**, there must be a word of negative meaning in the same clause. This word can be outside the verb phrase and may be a word with a negative sense, such as *only, never, hardly* ($\rightarrow$ 4).

As a modal verb, ***dare*** has forms as follows:

I **dare** not go.	I **dared** not go.
He **dare** not go.	He **dared** not go.
He **daren't** go.	

Dare I do it?	**Dared** I do it?
Dare he do it?	**Dared** he do it?
Daren't he do it?	

As a main verb, ***dare*** has forms as follows:

I **dare to do** it.	I **did** not **dare to do** it.
He **dares to do** it.	He **did** not **dare to do** it.
He **does** not **dare to do** it.	**Does** he **dare to do** it?
He **doesn't dare to do** it.	**Doesn't** he **dare to do** it?

- Either of the two forms of *dare* can be used for sentences that have much the same meaning ($\rightarrow$ 5). The forms can overlap and produce phrases that have a mixed modal and main verb pattern. It is possible to say either:

Dare he *do* that!	modal form
or *Does* he *dare to do* that!	main verb form
or *Does* he *dare do* that!	mixed form

As a modal verb, *need* has forms as follows:

I **need** not **go**.	**Need** I **go**?
He **need** not **go**.	**Need** he **go**?
He **needn't** go.	**Needn't** he go?

As a main verb, *need* has forms as follows:

I **need** it.	I **needed to do** it.
He **needs** it.	He **has needed to do** it.
I **do** not **need to go**.	I **did** not **need to do** it.
He **does** not **need to go**.	**Does** he **need to do** that?

Examples

1 **Need** Paul **go** now? **Dare** Helen **prevent** him?

2 **Dared** Peter confront the masked raider?

3 Louisa **doesn't need to know** what Peter **dares to do**.
   Does Paul **need to go** now?
   Paul **needs to go**.
   Daren't he **stay**?

4 He **need only** ask and I will tell him.
   No sensible driver **dare** risk that chance.

5 Anna **didn't dare to jump** off the high fence.
   Anna **dared not jump** off the high fence.
   Most other people **wouldn't dare jump** either.

Used to

The verb **used to** is a marginal modal verb. Unlike the other modal verbs, it is only found in the past tense. Therefore, when it is used with **do** to make negatives and questions, the form of the auxiliary verb is always **did**.

Used to is used as follows:
  – to describe an activity or a state in the past that happened many times in the past but about which we now have no certain knowledge (→ 1).
  – to refer to an activity or state that was true in the past but is no longer true (→ 2).

Used to takes the following forms:
  – the form **used to** is used with all subjects e.g. *I, we, you, he, she, it, they* (→ 3), (→ 5).
  – the form in short answers is always **used to** rather than **used** on its own (→ 7).

There are two forms for a negative:
  – **used + not + to + base form**:
                    used not to (→ 4), (→ 6).
  – **did not / didn't + use + to + base form**:
                    did not / didn't use to (→ 2).

There are two forms for a question:
  – **used + subject + to + base form**:
                    used he to... ? (→ 7).
  – **did + subject + use to + base form**:
                    did he use to...? (→ 8).

• Note that negative questions with **did** can have two forms: **did he not use to...?** or **didn't he use to...?**
  In negatives and questions the forms with **did** are used the most, especially in American English.

The common contracted negative form is: **didn't use to**
The rarer contracted negative form is : **usedn't to**

• Do not confuse **used to** + base form with **be used to** + **present participle**, where **used to** means *accustomed to* (→ 9).

1 Gerry always **used to** go for a run before breakfast.
   Peter **didn't use to** like skiing when I knew him.

2 I **used to** go fell walking but I stopped after my fall.
   Although we have played tennis a lot this year, we **did
   not use to** play at all before.
   You **didn't use to** drive! – No I didn't, but I learnt last
   year.
   Alan **did not use to** like the cinema but now he is a
   real cinema buff.

3 I **used to**   We **used to**
   You **used to**   You **used to**
   She **used to**   They **used to**

4 I **used not to** like yoghurt but I enjoy it now.

5 I **used to** live in New Zealand.
   He **used to** deliver papers but he owns the shop now.
   Nancy and Ronald **used to** live in California.

6 When she first came she **usedn't to** speak to anyone;
   now she is very friendly.
   We **usedn't to** believe that she was sincere.

7 **Used he to** smoke a lot? – Yes, he certainly **used to**.

8 **Did** they **use to** visit you often? – Mary **used to**.

9 They lived in India for a long time, so they **are used
   to eating** spicy food.

Phrasal Verbs

A **phrasal verb** is a main verb combined with either:
– an **adverb** ($\rightarrow$ 1),
– a **preposition** ($\rightarrow$ 2), or
– an **adverb + preposition** ($\rightarrow$ 3),
to make a new verb. The adverb or the preposition becomes part of the verb.

There are many verbs that are not phrasal verbs, even though they are followed by one of the above items ($\rightarrow$ 4). It is normallly not a phrasal verb if you can ask a question *how? where? when?* (or any question using a **WH-** word) about the main verb and get an answer beginning with a preposition. Example 4, therefore, does not show phrasal verbs:

*How did he come? **By car**.*
*Where did he bring his friends? **Up to my flat***.
*When did they leave? **After the party***.

In the examples in 5, however, the main verb has combined with another word to make a new verb with a new meaning. These are **phrasal verbs**. You cannot ask a question about these sentences with any **WH-** word, such as *How did he come? What did she bring? Where did they look?* and arrive at a sensible answer.

In examples 6 to 11, in the first sentence of each pair the verb does not make a new meaning by combining with a preposition, so it is not a phrasal verb. The second one of the pair *is* a phrasal verb.

Continued

1 **take off**   **give in**
   blow up   **break in**

2 **get at** (someone)   **pick on** (weaker children)

3 **put up with** (insults)   **get out of** (doing something)

4 He came **by** car.
   He brought all his friends **up** to my flat.
   They left **after** the party.

5 He **came by** a new camera.
   She **brought up** all her children to believe in God.
   They **looked after** their elderly parents for many
   years.

6 The wind **blew** the papers up the street.
   They **blew up** the old factory chimney.

7 He managed to **bring** the cases up the stairs.
   Why **bring** that subject **up** again?

8 He watched the balloon **go away** over the rooftops.
   Shall we **go away** on holiday to Tunisia next month?

9 This piece has **broken** off the edge of the plate.
   The two sides **broke off** discussions late last night.

10 I see all the Dick Francis books have **gone** off the
   shelves again.
   I've **gone off** eating meat.

11 I could feel the car **run** over the kerb with a jolt.
   Would you **run over** that point of grammar again?

Phrasal Verbs (ctd)

The three types of phrasal verb are as follows:

Type A. Verb plus adverb
Some Type A phrasal verbs have no object, i.e. they are **intransitive**. The sentence makes sense without any further addition to the verb ($\to$ 1).

Others do have an object, because the main verb is normally **transitive**, otherwise the sentence is not meaningful ($\to$ 2), ($\to$ 3).

If the object is a **noun**, many Type A phrasal verbs will allow the adverb to come either :
– before the object ($\to$ 2), or
– after the object ($\to$ 3).

If the object is a **pronoun**, it must come before the adverb ($\to$ 4).
Sometimes you can guess the meaning of these verbs from the meanings of the parts ($\to$ 5).
Sometimes you have to learn the new meanings, or use a dictionary ($\to$ 6).

Type B Verb plus preposition
Type B phrasal verbs always have an object. This is because prepositions always govern an object ($\to$ 7). Sometimes there are two objects – the object of the verb and the object of the preposition ($\to$ 8).

Type C Verb plus adverb and preposition
Type C phrasal verbs are a combination of the two previous kinds of verb. All the parts of a Type C phrasal verb come before the object ($\to$ 9).

- It is sometimes hard to tell adverbs and prepositions apart, because often the same word can be both a preposition and an adverb, depending on how it is used. For further information about prepositions see p. 194.

Continued

1   Mary **went away**.
    Helen **sat down**.
    The students **came back**.

2   I **picked up** *Jim* on my way home.
    He **blew out** *the candle*.
    She **washed up** *the dishes*.

3   I picked *Jim* **up** on my way home.
    He blew *the candle* **out**.
    She washed *the dishes* **up**.

4   I picked *him* up.
    He blew *it* out.
    She washed *them* up.

5   to **sit down** = sit + down
    to **go away** = go + away

6   to **make up** (an answer) = invent
    to **put on** (a show)   = mount
    to **work out** (a problem) = solve
    to **put up** (a visitor)   = accommodate

7   He **asked for** *his bill*.   He **asked for** *it*.
    She **listened to** *the doctor*. She **listened to** *him*.
    They **referred to** *our conversation*. They **referred to** *it*.

8   He **asked** *the waiter* **for** *the bill*.

9   We are **looking forward to** *our holiday / it*.
    Don't **put up with** *bad behaviour / it*.
    You must **look out for** *traffic wardens / them*.

Phrasal Verbs (ctd)

The following are examples of the three types of phrasal verb that are explained on p. 68.

Type A
Phrasal verbs made from a verb plus an adverb may be intransitive (do not take an object) or transitive (take an object).

Some phrasal verbs that do not take an object	*Some phrasal verbs that do take an object*
to break down	to blow something up
to carry on	to break something off
to fall down	to bring a child up
to get about	to bring a subject up
to get up	to catch somebody up
to give up	to clear something up
to go away	to close something down
to go off	to give something up
to go on	to leave something out
to grow up	to make something up
to hold on	to pick someone up

Type B
Phrasal verbs made from a verb plus a preposition are all transitive. They follow this pattern:

He asked for his bill.	*He asked for it.*
to add to something	to hope for something
to agree with someone	to insist on something
to apply for a job	to laugh at something
to approve of something	to listen to something
to arrive at a place	to look after someone
to ask for something	to look for something
to believe in something	to look into something
to belong to someone	to pay for something
to call on someone	to refer to something
to care for someone	to rely on someone
to come across something	to run into someone
to deal with something	to run over something

Some Type B. verbs are doubly transitive, since both the verb and the preposition can have an object. They follow this pattern:

He asked the waiter for his bill.
to **add** insult **to** injury
to **ask** a bystander **for** help
to **check** the facts **with** the project leader
to **pay** the cashier **for** one's purchases
to **refer** an enquirer **to** the manager

Type C

Phrasal verbs with an adverb plus a preposition all take a prepositional object. They follow this pattern:
We are looking forward to our holiday.
We are looking forward to it.

to be fed up with something
to break in on someone
to carry on with something
to catch up with something
to check up on something
to come up with something
to cut down on something
to do away with something
to face up to something
to fall back on something
to get on with someone
to get out of something
to go back on something
to go in for something
to keep away from something
to lead up to something
to look back on something
to look forward to something
to look out for something
to look up to someone
to make up for something
to put in for something
to run away with something
to run out of something
to run up against something
to stand up for something
to walk out on someone
to watch out for something

Tense

Time reference

We need to be able to refer to time in sentences. **Tense** is the name given to the way verb forms help us make time reference. We can state whether an action or a state took place in the past or in the present ($\rightarrow$ 1).

There are two **simple tenses** and six **compound tenses**.

Simple tenses

The simple tenses are so called because they consist of a single word, a **main verb**.

There is a **Simple Present** tense ($\rightarrow$ 2) and a **Simple Past** tense ($\rightarrow$ 3).

The simple tenses of regular verbs

The **Present** tense is the same as the **base form** of the verb, except that an **-s** is added to the verb when it takes a noun or *he, she,* or *it* as a subject. This is called the 3rd person singular form ($\rightarrow$ 4).

The **Past** tense of a regular verb is made from the **base form** of the verb with **-ed** added. The spelling is the same for all persons ($\rightarrow$ 3).

The simple tenses of irregular verbs

Most irregular verbs make the **Present tense** from the **base form** of the verb just as regular verbs do ($\rightarrow$ 5).

- Irregular verbs make the **Past tense** in a number of different ways. Sometimes the past tense is a quite different word ($\rightarrow$ 6). See pp. 24–25 for more on irregular verbs.

1 Nadia **hopes** to get three grade A passes in her exams
   next month.
   Jessica **works** in the general office.
   Lance **worked** for the Post Office in his vacation.
   Terry **opened** a new bank account.

2 I **like**   I **live**
   you **like**   you **live**
   he **likes**   he **lives**

3 I **liked**   I **lived**
   you **liked**   you **lived**
   he **liked**   he **lived**

4 he / she / it **likes**
   he / she / it **lives**

5 *Present*
   I **find**   I **go**
   you **find**   you **go**
   he **finds**   he **goes**

6 *Past*
   I **found**   I **went**
   you **found**   you **went**
   he **found**   he **went**

Aspect

When we use a verb, we need to be able to refer to more than the time at which an event took place. We need to be able to refer to actions and states as completed or not completed. **Aspect** describes the way we think of verbal actions.

We use **progressive aspect** to show that an action:
– is going on at the time of speaking (→ 1).
– was going on throughout the time that you are referring to (→ 2).
– will be going on at the time that you are referring to (→ 3). This can also refer to a possible future event.

The **progressive aspect** is formed by using the appropriate form of the auxiliary *be* together with the *-ing* form (**present participle**) of the main verb (→ 1), (→ 2), (→ 3).

We use **perfect aspect** to show that an action:
– is complete at the time of speaking (→ 4).
– was complete at the time you are referring to (→ 5).

The **perfect aspect** is formed by using the appropriate form of the auxiliary *have* together with the *-ed* form (**past participle**) of the main verb (→ 4), (→ 5).

• Simple tenses do not show an aspect. It is possible to have a compound tense that shows both aspects (→ 6), progressive and perfect.

1 I **am using** a word processor.
  I know that you **are reading** this sentence.
  Mr Wheeler **is whistling** as he polishes his car.

2 A few minutes ago he **was washing** his car.
  I **was waiting** for her as she finished work.
  We **were eating** out that night.

3 We **are going** to Turkey for a holiday next year.
  They **are coming** to us for Christmas this year.

4 I **have finished** his latest novel now.
  Both of us **have enjoyed** it very much.
  Jo **has borrowed** the book until Sunday afternoon.

5 I **had forgotten** my promise to Aunt Jane.
  Shirley **had lost** her key, so she had to wait until Alan
  came back.
  Bill and Sue **had seen** the film three times already.

6 Peter **has been visiting** his oldest friend recently.

Compound Tenses

The compound tenses are so called because they consist of
a **main verb** plus one or more **auxiliary verbs**. Each
compound tense contains a part that makes the tense
either present or past, and a part that makes the aspect
either progressive or perfect ($\rightarrow 1$), ($\rightarrow 2$).
See also pp. 14–18.

The compound tenses are a combination of present or past
tense with progressive or perfect **aspect**.

• The tense of the auxiliary verb shows whether the
  compound verb is **present** tense ($\rightarrow 1$), or **past** tense ($\rightarrow 2$).

The choice of the **auxiliary** and the **participle** shows what
aspect the verb has.
– if it is the auxiliary *be* and the *-ing* participle (the
  present participle) the aspect is **progressive** ($\rightarrow 3$), ($\rightarrow 4$).
– if it is the auxiliary *have* and the *-ed* participle (the
  past participle) the aspect is **perfect** ($\rightarrow 5$), ($\rightarrow 6$).

These are the possible combinations:
Present Progressive = present of *be* + *-ing*
                         participle ($\rightarrow 3$).
Past Progressive   = past of *be* + *-ing* participle ($\rightarrow 4$).
Present Perfect   = present of *have* + *-ed*
                         participle ($\rightarrow 5$).
Past Perfect   = past of *have* + *-ed* participle ($\rightarrow 6$).

A compound verb can also combine both the progressive
and perfect aspects, using **two auxiliary verbs** and a
main verb. This produces the following combinations:

Present Perfect Progressive
    = present of *have* + past participle of *be* + *-ing*
       participle ($\rightarrow 7$).
Past Perfect Progressive
    = past of *have* + past participle of *be* + *-ing*
       participle ($\rightarrow 8$).

Continued

1 I **am writing** a letter at the moment, so I can't come.
Frank **has seen** the camera that he wants.

2 She **was preparing** a meal as she listened to the radio.
Sandra **had invited** all her friends.

3 My brother **is having** a party tomorrow.
Kerry **is waiting** until her friend Jessica comes.

4 They **were running** wild all over the place before we
weeded them out.
Marcia **was watching** an old film on TV when Jo
called.

5 Jill **has walked** more than 500 miles for charity.
Lennie **has seen** several things that he likes.
He **has bought** some better equipment.

6 Bobbie **had really believed** what she was told.
The old man **had tied up** the dog to stop it wandering
away.
Rodney **had had** enough of this interference in his
affairs.

7 For the past two months, Zia **has been visiting** his
elderly uncle.
We **have been trying** to finish that job since before
Easter.

8 Marlene **had been hoping** for better news than the
letter gave her.
I **had been sleeping** before the telephone rang.

Compound Tenses (ctd)

The modal auxiliaries can be used in compound tenses ($\rightarrow$ 1). They are either used alone or followed by the base forms *have* or *be*.

They come first in the verb phrase, so they are followed by:
– the subject and the rest of the verb in questions ($\rightarrow$ 2).
– the negative *not* and the rest of the verb in negative statements ($\rightarrow$ 3).
– the subject, the negative *not*, and the rest of the verb in negative questions ($\rightarrow$ 4). If the contracted negative form of the modal is used then it comes before the subject and and the rest of the verb ($\rightarrow$ 5).

• Modals are not used in Simple tenses.

• Modals are not used with the supporting auxiliary verb *do*.

See pp. 44–65 for the meanings and uses of modal auxiliary verbs.

Responses

You usually use just the first part of the verb phrase in a compound verb as the response form. That is, you use one of the auxiliary verbs. If it is a Simple tense you use the supporting auxiliary *do* ($\rightarrow$ 6). If one of the forms of *be* or *have* is the first verb in the verb phrase, then use that as the response form ($\rightarrow$ 7). If a **modal** verb is first in the verb phrase, some speakers prefer to use the modal and the auxiliary form together as the response form ($\rightarrow$ 8).

Other compound verb forms

Other compound verb forms are made by choosing the **passive** rather than the **active voice** in a sentence. See pp. 106–111 for more on the passive voice.

1 She **might be seeing** her boyfriend on Friday.
   Larry **would be sitting** here every Friday in the old days.
   I **may have eaten** something which disagreed with me.
   Nayeema **will have bought** something for our supper.

2 **Will you be doing** some shopping?

3 Marcus **may not have been** entirely truthful.

4 **Will he not be calling** on Marcia this evening?

5 **Won't** he **be calling** on Marcia this evening?

6 **Do** you **like** courgettes? – Yes, I **do**.

7 **Has** Tammy called round yet? – Yes, she **has**.
   Was Nayeema calling? – Yes, she **was**.

8 **Might** he **have left** the parcel somewhere? – Yes, he **might** or Yes, he **might have**.
   Laurence **could be coming** with us then. – Yes, he **could** or Yes, he **could be**.

The Simple Present Tense

Typical forms of this tense are as in example 1. Because the Simple Present consists of one word only, the Simple Present tense of *do* is used as the supporting auxiliary when you want to ask a question (→ 2), make a negative statement using *not* (→ 3), or make a response (→ 4).

We use the Simple Present tense to talk about:
– habits or things that happen regularly (→ 5). (When we talk about habits, we often add adverbs such as *often, always, usually, sometimes,* or *never*, or adverbial phrases such as *on Sundays* or *in the summer*).
– statements of fact that are scientific truths or that are about a permanent state (→ 6).
– statements that indicate the speaker's general belief or feeling (→ 7).

We sometimes choose the Simple Present for dramatic narrative to tell a story or describe an action vividly (→ 8), for example when giving a commentary on a sports event or public function (→ 9).

● We can also use the Simple Present for planned future actions with a time adverb, for example to talk about travel plans (→ 10). See p. 96 to p. 105 for more about future reference.

● We use the Simple Present in conditional sentences about real possibilities that affect the future (→ 11). See p. 240 for more on conditional sentences.

1 I walk.   He walks.

2 **Do** I walk?   **Does** she walk?

3 I **do not** walk.
   She **does not** walk.

4 **Do** you just **have** coffee for breakfast? – Yes, I **do**

5 I **like** coffee for breakfast but my flatmate **prefers** tea.
   I **don't take** sugar in my coffee.
   What **does** Jamie **usually eat** for breakfast?
   They **often go** to a football match **on Saturdays**.
   I **don't usually watch** football.

6 The sun **rises** in the east.
   Birds **fly**.
   We **live** in Scotland.

7 I **believe** that he is a very good teacher.
   I **don't like** horror films.

8 He **walks** slowly to the checkout and **puts** his bag on
   the counter. As the cashier **opens** the till he **draws** a
   gun . . .

9 . . . but Becker **sees** it. He **runs** up to the net and
   smashes the ball.

10 We **leave** by train at 10.40 a.m. on Monday and **arrive**
   at 3.30 p.m.

11 If I **lend** you my notes, I won't be able to revise
   tonight.

The Simple Past Tense

Typical forms of this tense are as in example 1. Because
the Simple Past consists of one word only, the Simple Past
tense of *do*, which is *did*, is used as the supporting
auxiliary when you want to ask a question (→ 2), make a
negative statement using *not* (→ 3), or make a response
(→ 4).

We use the Simple Past tense to talk about:
– single actions in the past (→ 5).
– habitual actions in the past, often with *always, never,* or
  often (→ 6).
– past actions where a definite time is mentioned. It is often
  used with a time expression such as *ago* or *last month*,
  when the action is seen as finished (→ 7).
– points where the main action is broken or when an
  action goes on during or alongside another. The rest of the
  sentence uses the Past Progressive tense to describe the
  past activity or action (→ 8), (→ 9).

• You can instead use two Simple Past verbs to
  indicate an action which goes on during or alongside
  another (→ 10).

1 I **looked**.   She **looked**.
   I **went**.   She **went**.

2 **Did** I **look**?   **Did** she **look**?
   Did I **go**?   **Did** it **go**?

3 I **did** not **look**.   He **did** not **look**.
   I **did** not **go**.   He **did** not **go**.

4 **Did** you **see** Jenny yesterday? – No, I **didn't**.
   Did Jenny **phone** you ? – Yes, she **did**.

5 He **locked** the door and **left** the house.
   I just **walked** out and **brought** the cat back in again.

6 In those days I **always went** to Respighi's for lunch.
   I **cycled in daily** and that soon **made** me fit.
   I **often visited** Glasgow on business but never as a
   tourist.

7 **Some time ago** now, I **went** to America for a month.
   Once upon a time a king in a far land **opened** a box.
   I **saw** Roger **a little while back**.
   I **bought** the microwave **a year ago**.

8 I was clearing out the stable when a car **came** down
   the drive.
   We were leaving to go to dinner when the phone **rang**.

9 Helen was reading the paper while the lunch **cooked**.
   Peter was watching television as he **ironed** his shirts.

10 Helen **read** the paper while the lunch **cooked**.
   Peter **watched** television as he **ironed** his shirts.

The Present Progressive Tense

Typical forms of this tense are as in examples 1, 2, and 3.

Some main verbs are not normally used in the progressive in standard British English, though they may be used this way in other varieties of English. These are generally verbs about states rather than actions (→ 4).

We use the Present Progressive tense to talk about:
– things that are happening now, at the time when we are talking (→ 5). When you give a short answer to a question, it is normal to echo the auxiliary but not the main verb (→ 6).
– a temporary activity even if it is not happening at the time when we are talking (→ 7).
– a temporary situation in contrast to a permanent situation (→ 8).
– a changing state or situation (→ 9).
– a situation that can happen at any time (→ 10).
– future events along with a time adverb or phrase (→ 11). See p. 96 for more on the future.

We also use it to express annoyance. In this case one of the following adverbs is used with the verb: *always, forever, constantly, continually* (→ 12).

1 I am writing.   He is writing

2 Am I listening?
   Is she listening?

3 I am not writing.   He is not writing.
   Aren't I listening?   Isn't she listening?
   Am I not listening?   Is she not listening?

4 I am listening.
   She is listening   *but not*: *I am liking it.*
   I am not listening.
   She is not listening   *but not*: *I am not liking it.*

5 Mother's **making** supper, I'm **doing** my homework,
   but Jenny **isn't doing** anything.
   The children aren't asleep, they're **talking** quietly.
   It's not true. Fergus **isn't clinging** to the past.

6 **Are** you **waiting** for someone? – Yes, I **am**.
   Is Hamish **working** in the library? – No, he **isn't**.

7 I **am studying** German at college this year.
   I'm **putting** a deposit on a new car.

8 I **am living** in Scotland **for the present**.
   My mother lives in London but she **is visiting** Paris
   this weekend.

9 My headache **is getting** better.
   The daylight **is slowly fading**.

10 I wear my glasses **when I'm reading**.

11 I **am flying** to New York **next week**.

12 She's **always coming** in late at night and **disturbing**
   everyone.

The Past Progressive Tense

Typical forms of this tense are as shown in examples 1, 2, and 3.

Some main verbs are not normally used in the progressive in standard British English, though they may be used this way in other varieties of English. These are generally verbs about states rather than feelings.

We use the Past Progressive tense in these ways:
- with a time expression, such as *at 6p.m. yesterday*, to talk about an action that began before that time and finished after it. The exact length of time the action took is not important ($\rightarrow$ 4).
- to talk about a longer action in contrast to a shorter action in the past. Note that for the shorter action we use the Simple Past tense ($\rightarrow$ 5).
- to describe a scene in the past, especially in a story ($\rightarrow$ 6).
- to talk about slow or gradual action in the past ($\rightarrow$ 7).
- to talk about two or more longer actions which took place over the same period of time in the past ($\rightarrow$ 8).

1 I was listening   ***but not***: *I was liking it.*
   She was listening.
   They were listening.

2 Am I listening?
   Is she listening?
   Were you listening?

3 I was not talking   ***but not***: *I was not liking it.*
   We were not talking.
   They weren't trying.
   I wasn't trying either.

4 I **was standing** at the bus stop at eight o'clock. An
   hour later I **was typing** in the office.

5 While I **was waiting** for the bus I **dropped** my purse.
   Saïd **was still standing** in the queue when the film
   began.
   You **were not sitting** in your places when the bell
   rang.

6 It was a dreadful morning. The snow **was still falling**,
   the wind **was blowing**, and the cars **were skidding**
   on the icy roads.

7 The sun **was rising**.
   He made some tea while the toast **was cooling**.
   The convoy **was winding** its way through the tangled
   country lanes.

8 They **were all working** in the garden. Jim **was
   mowing** the grass, John **was cutting** the hedge, and
   David **was weeding** the flowerbeds.

The Present Perfect Tense

Typical forms of this tense are as shown in examples 1, 2, and 3.

The contracted forms are:

has = **'s**	have = **'ve**
has not = **hasn't**	have not = **haven't**

The Present Perfect tense is used to talk about events that are relevant to the present but that happened in the past.

It is used to talk about an action that started, or that failed to start, in the past, without mentioning a specific time (→ 4). If *have* occurs more than once in a compound sentence, all but the first instance may be left out (→ 5).

- We can use *just* if we want to show that the action has very recently been completed (→ 6). If the event did not take place you can use *never*. If you want to check if it did take place, you can use *ever* (→ 7).

- If we want to talk about a moment in time or a period of time, we can use expressions such as *recently, lately, this morning, today*, or *this week* with the Present Perfect tense (→ 8).

- In questions and negative sentences the Present Perfect can be used with *yet*, meaning 'at the time of speaking' (→ 9).

The Present Perfect tense is often used with an optional time adverbial (→ 10). See pp. 172–174. It is used to answer the question *How long...?* together with *for* to talk about a period of time, or *since* to talk about duration from a point in time (→ 11).

1 I have **finished**.   He **has found** them.
   They've **finished**.   They've **found** her.
   Listen! I've **heard** the most exciting news; Jim's **won**!
   They've **bought** a brand new car.
   You've **got** a nerve!

2 **Have** they **finished**? – No, they **haven't**.
   Has Mary **arrived** yet? – No, she **hasn't**.

3 I have not **finished**.   He has not **finished**.
   Ranee **hasn't found** her bracelet yet.
   They **haven't seen** her.

4 Her daughter **has fallen** ill.
   We **have seen** the waxworks at Madame Tussaud's.

5 They **have bought** their tickets and **booked** seats.

6 They **have just bought** their tickets.
   He **has just finished** his homework.

7 **Have** you **ever been** to Greece? – No, I **have never
   been** there.

8 I **have not been** to the cinema **recently**.
   I **have waited a week** for your answer.

9 **Haven't** you **finished yet**?
   Have you **bought** the tickets **yet**?

10 He **has been** here **frequently**.
   I **have always lived** in London.
   He **has worked** at Collins **all his life**.

11 I **have lived** in Edinburgh **for** fifteen years.
   How long **have you lived** in Edinburgh? – **Since** 1986.
   We **haven't spoken** to each other **since** we quarrelled.

The Past Perfect Tense

Typical forms of this tense are as shown in examples 1, 2, and 3.

The contracted forms are:
    had = 'd   had not = **hadn't**

The Past Perfect tense goes one step further back into the past than the Present Perfect ($\rightarrow$ 4). Like all Perfect tenses, it deals with actions or states that are seen as having a finishing point.

Just as the Present Perfect tense is used to talk about a recently completed action ($\rightarrow$ 5), the Past Perfect tense is used to talk about an action that took place in the past before something else took place ($\rightarrow$ 6).

- The Past Perfect is not often used in questions, since it refers to a period of past time about which all doubts have normally been resolved. It is more often used in the main clause of a complex sentence ($\rightarrow$ 6), to set the scene for an event.

- The Past Perfect tense is used with a time expression such as *always* or *for several days* to talk about an action that began before another action in the past and continued up to the time of the second action ($\rightarrow$ 7) and perhaps even beyond that time ($\rightarrow$ 8).

1 I **had gone**.   She **had gone**.
   I **had finished**.   She **had found** them.
   She**'d gone**.   They**'d found** her.

2 **Had** I **gone**?   **Had** it **gone**?
   Had Mary **arrived** before Peter told you? – No, she
   hadn't.

3 I **had** not **gone**.   He **had gone**.
   I **had** not **finished**.   It **had** not **worked**.
   I **hadn't seen** the Oscar ceremony on television; **I'd
   gone** to bed early that night.
   They **hadn't seen** her.

4 **Had** you ever **seen** her before then? – No, I **hadn't**.

5 *Compare with 6*
   I **have just made** some fresh coffee. Would you like
   some?

6 *Compare with 5*
   She **had just made** some coffee when I arrived, so I
   stayed and drank a cup.

7 We **had wanted** to visit Canada **for a long time**, so
   last year we went there for our holiday.

8 Ashraf **had known** my brother **for two years** before I
   met him.

The Present Perfect Progressive Tense

Typical forms of this tense are as shown in examples 1, 2, and 3.

We use the Present Perfect Progressive tense to talk about actions and states that began in the past and are still continuing at the time of speaking (→ 4), or have only just finished (→ 5). It is also used for repeated actions (→ 6).

There is sometimes little difference between the meaning of the Present Perfect and the meaning of the Present Perfect Progressive when they are used for long-term actions (→ 7). We usually choose the progressive form for more temporary actions or states (→ 8) and the Present Perfect form for more permanent ones (→ 9).

- We cannot use this tense with verbs such as *be, know,* and *like,* which are not used in progressive forms.

- We can use *for* and *since* with the progressive form in the same way as with the Present Perfect form (→ 7), (→ 8), (→ 9). See also pp.84–86 for more about progressive uses of the verb.

1 I have been waiting.   I've been waiting.
   She has been waiting. She's been waiting.

2 Have I been waiting? Yes, I have!
   Has he been waiting? – No, he hasn't.
   Have you been waiting long?

3 I have not been waiting.
   She has not been waiting.

4 I have been holding this ladder for half an hour now.
   When are you going to come down?

5 There you are! I have been waiting for hours!

6 I have been buying my papers here for a year.

7 *Compare:*
   I have been studying English for three years but I
   still can't understand what gerunds are.
   I have studied English for three years but I still can't
   understand what gerunds are.

8 I have been living in London since I started work.

9 I have lived in London since birth.

The Past Perfect Progressive Tense

Typical forms of this tense are as shown in examples 1, 2, and 3.

The Past Perfect Progressive tense is used to talk about an action which began before another action in the past and either:
- continued up to the time of the second action ($\to$ 4), or
- was completed before the second action happened ($\to$ 5).

The Past Perfect can be used in the same way. See p. 90. It is often possible to use either tense with little difference in meaning ($\to$ 6), ($\to$ 7).

- The Past Perfect Progressive is not often used in questions, since it refers to a period of past time about which all doubts have normally been resolved. It is more often used in the main clause of a complex sentence ($\to$ 4), to set the scene for an event.

- The Past Perfect Progressive is often used to talk about a repeated action ($\to$ 8).

- Remember that you cannot use the Past Perfect Progressive with verbs such as *like*, which are not used in the progressive. See p. 84.

1 I **had been waiting**.   I'**d been waiting**.
   She **had been waiting**. She'**d been waiting.**

2 **Had** I **been waiting** long, she asked.
   Had he **been waiting**?
   Had you been expecting to meet Mary at the
   station? No, I **hadn't**. She usually takes a later train.

3 I **had not been waiting**.
   She **had not been waiting**.
   They **hadn't been looking** very carefully.

4 My car broke down, so I got out and stood by the road.
   I **hadn't been waiting** long when a lorry drew up
   beside me.
   She **had been looking** at the parcel for some time
   before she realized that it was for her sister.

5 I **had been studying** and decided to take a stroll to
   clear my mind.
   We **had been cleaning** the car for hours, so we felt
   quite pleased with ourselves.

6 I **had been driving** for about an hour when I **heard** a
   noise in the engine.

7 I **had driven** for about an hour when I **heard** a noise
   in the engine.

8   She **had been trying** to telephone her mother all day.

Future Reference

Verb forms

English has no future tense of the verb as such. However, several forms and certain set groups of the verb, especially the **modal** verbs *will* and *shall*, can be used to make future reference. These forms are summarized as follows:

1   *will / shall* + the base form makes the most direct form of future reference (→ 1). See p. 98. The other modal verbs that express possibility make a more indirect reference to future time.

2   *be going to* + the base form is used to express intention and make predictions (→ 2). See p. 100.

3   **The Present Progressive tense** is used to talk about plans and arrangements in the future with a time adverb (→ 3). See p. 102.

4   **The Simple Present tense** is used with a time adverb to talk about future plans which are part of a timetable or previous arrangement (→ 4). See p. 102.

5   **The Future Perfect tense** (*will have* + the **past participle**) is used with a time adverb to talk about an action that will be finished at the time in the future that you are referring to (→ 5). See p. 102.

6   *be about to* + the base form is used to talk about the very near future (→ 6). See p.102.

7   **The Future Progressive tense** (*will be* + the **present participle**) is used to talk about future action in progress (→ 7). See p. 104.

8   *be to* + the base form is used to talk about formal plans (→ 8). See p. 104.

Continued

1 It **will take** several years to finish.
   Jean **will look after** the dogs while we're away.
   I **shall** simply **tell** her to mind her own business.
   We **shall see**.

2 He failed his exam last year; this year he **is going to work** harder.
   You'd better take the washing in; it **is going to rain**.

3 Sarah and Harriet **are meeting at ten o'clock** on **Tuesday**.
   I **am flying** to Glasgow **on Friday**.

4 The main film **starts at 2.45 p.m.**
   We **leave at 4 p.m. tomorrow**.

5 I was hoping to meet James, but by the time I arrive he **will have gone** home.

6 I'm sorry I can't stop and chat; **I'm just about to leave** for work.

7 What **will** you **be doing** on Saturday? Oh, **I'll be shopping** as usual.

8 The Queen **is to attend** the ceremony.

Future Reference (ctd)

will
shall

The modal verbs *will* or *shall* followed by the **base form** of a main verb are used to express future reference (→ 1).

Will can be used with all persons of the verb, although some speakers prefer to use *shall* in the first person singular and plural. See p.54 for further details.

- The contracted form is *'ll* for both verbs, so there is no difference in informal speech (→ 2). The contracted negative forms are *won't* and *shan't* (→ 3).
- If there are two verbs in the sentence, it is normal not to repeat the modal form before the second one (→ 7).

We use *will* (or *shall*) for future reference in the following ways:
- to express a firm intention (→ 4).
- to announce an action that the speaker has just decided on (→ 5).
- to express negative intention, using *won't*. In the first person, *shan't* is an alternative (→ 6).
- to talk about an event in the future, possibly in the distant future (→ 7). A time clause may or may not be used.
- to refer to inevitable actions or events that will take place in the future (→ 8).
- to express an opinion about a future event after verbs such as *believe, expect, hope, know,* and *think* (→ 9).
- to express a real possibility in conditional sentences (→ 10). See p. 240.

Continued

1 I **shall come**.   We **shall come**.
   or   *or*
   I **will come**.   We **will come**.
   You **will come**.   You **will come**.
   She / he / it **will come**.   They **will come**.

2 I**'ll come** by train, but they**'ll come** by car.

3 We **shan't come**.   We **won't come**.

4 **I'll be** home in time for supper.
   I shan't see Mary next week.

5 Right then. We **will meet** again on Monday.

6 This **won't happen** again, I can assure you.
   She was very rude to me so I **won't invite** her.
   I shan't buy my vegetables there again.

7 People **will look** at these pictures and **know** how we
   dressed in 1990's.

8 Christmas is past, but it **will come** again next year.
   The daffodils **will flower** in the Spring.

9 I expect he **will be** home soon.

10 If you phone after six **I'll tell** you.

Future Reference (ctd)

be going to
Future reference can be made with **be** + **going to** + the
base form of a main verb (→ 1).

Be going to is used in the following ways:
– to express intention about the future (→ 2).
– to talk about things that we have already decided (→ 3).
– to make a prediction about the future, often the very
  near future, based on something in the present (→ 4).
– if the past tense of **be** is used, a past intention or
  prediction can be expressed (→ 5).

• Note this difference:
  Be going to is usually used for future events where the
  speaker expresses his or her intention.
  Will is used as a more neutral expression (→ 6) .
  In the first and fourth lines of example 6, the speaker
  is expressing an intention. In the second and third lines,
  the speaker is agreeing to someone else's arrangements.
  The forms under discussion could not be exchanged in
  these examples.

Continued

1   I **am going to wait**.   He **is going to wait**.
    I **am not going to wait**.He **is not going to wait**.
    Is he **going to wait**?   **Are** they **going to wait**?

2   Mary **isn't going** to study art; she**'s going** to be a
    nurse.

3   Is Jim **going to share** your flat? – Yes, **he is**.
    Where's Mary? She said she **was going to come** early.

4   Watch the milk! It **is going to boil** over!
    Sally never does any work; she **is going to fail** her
    exams.

5   Judy **was going to meet** me, but she was ill and
    couldn't come.
    She **was** obviously **going to get** blisters with those
    new shoes.

6   I**'m going to go** to the pictures on Friday; would you
    like to come?
    Yes, I**'ll come**.
    I**'ll go** if you go; Peter **will come** too if you ask him.
    Peter, **are** you **going to** join us?

Future Reference (ctd)

Present Progressive

The Present Progressive tense is used to talk about plans
for the future or specific arrangements that people have
made for future events (→ 1). It is often used in questions
about future arrangements (→ 2). If there are two verbs in
the sentence, it is normal not to repeat the modal form
before the second one (→ 3).

Simple Present

The Simple Present tense is also used to talk about plans,
but is mostly used for events that form part of a timetable
or programme (→ 4).

The Future Perfect (*will have* + the past participle of a main verb).

This form is used to talk about an action that will be
complete at a time in the future that you are talking
about. It is often used with the main verb *finish* or
complete.

The contracted positive form is *'ll have* or *will've* (→ 5).
The contracted negative is *won't have* (→ 6). In questions
the subject comes after *will* (→ 7). The short answer to a
question is *will* or *will have* without the past participle (→ 7).

be + about to + the base form

The appropriate form of *be* + *about to* + the base form
of a main verb is used to talk about events in the very
near future (→ 8). It is sometimes used with *just* following
the *be* word to give even more immediacy (→ 9).

Be about to can also be used in the past to suggest that
someone was *on the point of* carrying out an action. In this
case it is usually followed by *when* (→ 10).

Continued

1 The church **is having** a sale next week; **I'm running** the bookstall.

2 What **are you doing** on Saturday? – **I'm going** to a football match with Peter.
When **are you leaving**? – At the end of term.

3 We **are meeting** at 12.30 p.m., **having** a quick lunch, and **starting** work at 1.15.

4 The train **leaves** Edinburgh at 10.10 a.m. and **reaches** London at 3.20 p.m.
These are the arrangements for Friday: the doors **open** at 7 p.m., the Mayor **arrives** at 7.30 p.m., and the meeting **starts** at 7.45 p.m.

5 Can you come skiing next Saturday? – Yes, I can. **I'll have finished** my exams by then.
He **will've made** some sandwiches by the time we get back, so we can all go for a picnic.

6 David's essay is due on Tuesday, but **he won't have completed** it by then. He **won't** even **have read** all the books!

7 **Will** you **have collected** all the details before the next meeting? – Yes, **I will (have)**.

8 Turn off the gas – the soup **is about to boil** over.
We **were about to go** into the cinema when he joined us.

9 Quick, jump in! The train **is (just) about to leave**.

10 They **were (just) about to go** to bed **when** the phone rang.

Future Reference (ctd)

The Future Progressive Tense
This is made with *will* + *be* + the **present participle** of a main verb. The verb group *will be* forms negatives, contractions, questions, and short answers in the usual way.

The Future Progressive is used in a rather informal way to suggest that something is about to happen or will happen at some time that is not clear or precise (→ 1).It is also used to indicate normal future reference, especially when you wish to talk about a process that is about to take place (→ 2).

- Compare: They **will call** us on Monday – They **will be calling** us on Monday.
  The latter is less formal.

be to + the base form
The appropriate form of *be* + *to* + the base form of a main verb is used mainly in fairly formal English to talk about plans, arrangements, and instructions. It indicates that what will happen is part of an expected process (→ 3).

- Compare: They **will call** us on Monday – They **are to call** us on Monday.
  The latter suggests that they are obliged to do something and is much more formal.

1 I'll **be seeing** you.
   We'll **be getting** in touch with you.
   They'll **be wanting** us to clean our own classrooms
   next.
   We **won't be seeing** Uncle John while we are in
   Australia.

2 **Will** you **be working** in the burger bar next week?
   No, I won't. **I'll be starting** my new job.
   Just think! Next Wednesday we **will be flying** to
   Sydney.

3 The two representatives **are to meet** in order to
   discuss the agenda for future action.
   The President has left for Geneva, where he **is to**
   attend the talks.

Active and Passive Voice

We talk about the **voice** of a sentence in order to say
something about the relationship between:
– the **verb** in a clause,
– the **subject** of the verb,
– the person or thing that does the verbal action,
– the person or thing that the verbal action is done to.

Active Voice

In example 1 the verb is in the **active voice**. The subject
of an active-voice sentence is also the person or thing that
carries out the action that the verb expresses. We use the
active voice when the subject of the verb is the doer of the
action. The active voice is used in most English speech and
writing, because we usually want to inform our listener or
our reader who or what carried out the action of the verb
($\rightarrow$ 2).

Passive Voice

In example 3 the verb is in the **passive voice**. The subject
in a passive-voice sentence is not the person or thing that
does the action of the verb. It is the person or thing that is
acted on by the verb ($\rightarrow$ 4).

- We use the passive voice to direct our listener's
  attention to the important part of our message.
  For instance, in example 3 we do not need to know who
  delivers the letters, so all mention of the postman is left
  out.

- The passive voice can be used when we do not know
  who carries out the action expressed by the verb, or
  when it is not important that we should know. It is
  sometimes much more important to know what has
  happened than who or what did it ($\rightarrow$ 5).

Continued

1 **The postman delivers** letters every day.

2 **He hid** the money under the bed.
   The car knocked over a pedestrian.
   The publishers are sending the book from London.

3 **Letters are delivered** every day.

4 **The injured man was helped** by a passer-by.
   The horse was being ridden by a young woman.
   The patient was operated on by a famous surgeon.

5 The money **was hidden** under the bed.
   The book **is being sent** from London.
   An elderly man **was run over** crossing the road.
   Roger **has been given** his promotion.
   The patient **was operated on.**
   Jake's old car **was sold.**

Passive Voice (ctd)

The passive allows us to select the parts of a sentence to which we want to draw attention. It can be used when we want to focus on:
– the **agent**, i.e. who brought the action about. We show the agent with *by* (→ 1).
– the **instrument**, i.e. what was used to make the action happen. We show the instrument with *by* or *with* (→ 2).
– the **means**, i.e. what caused the action to happen. We show the means with *by* or *with* (→ 3).

The subject of a passive verb

The verb in a passive sentence has the word that would normally be its object in the position of the subject. When a verb has two objects, either the indirect object or the direct object of the active verb may become the subject of the passive verb (→ 4). If the indirect object is mentioned after the passive verb, the sentence must use *to* (→ 5). Some verbs that are often used this way are: *give, offer, lend, promise, sell,* and *tell*.

Form of the passive

Passive verbs are made from a form of *be* + the **past participle** of a main verb. In the passive voice, the form of the auxiliary verb *be* indicates the tense (→ 6).

• There is a small group of words that are only or mostly used in the passive, e.g. *be born* and *be drowned*, where it is normally something that happens to you rather than something that someone does to you (→ 7).

Continued

1   The window was broken **by some boys who were throwing stones**.
    My brother was given extra tuition **by his teacher**.
    The old man was run over **by a careless driver**.
    The patient was operated on **by a team of top surgeons**.

2   The window was broken **by a stone** which was thrown up **by a passing car**.
    The safe was blown open **with a stick of dynamite**.
    The old man was knocked over **by a bus**.
    The patient was dosed **with painkiller** to make him drowsy.

3   The window was shattered **by an explosion**.
    He was exhausted **with the strain of caring for his injured friend**.
    The passage for study was marked **with a cross in the margin**.
    He was taken to hospital **by ambulance**.

4   **Henry was sold** Jake's old car.
    Ruari was given my copy of *Great Expectations* by Philippa.

5   Jake's old car **was sold to** Henry.
    My copy of *Great Expectations* **was given to** Ruari.

6   They **sell** fresh vegetables in this market.
    Fresh vegetables **are sold** in this market.
    They once **sold** live poultry in this market.
    At one time live poultry **was sold** in this market.

7   Which king **was drowned** in the Wash?
    The Captain **was born** in Wales.

Passive Voice (ctd)

The impersonal passive

This form of passive sentence is useful when you want to report what is or was generally understood or accepted by a group of people (→ 1). It has the form: *it* + **passive.**
The impersonal passive can be used when you do not want to mention the source of a report or rumour (→ 2).

The passive with *get*

In informal spoken English, a type of passive is sometimes made with *get* instead of *be* (→ 3).
It is usually used to talk about something that just happens or that is done by someone to himself or herself, rather than being done by another person, e.g. *get dressed, get lost, get washed.*

The causative passive with *have*

There is another kind of verbal group that is like the passive, because the person who carries out the action of the main verb is not the person who is the subject of the clause (→ 4). It expresses the idea that the subject caused or ordered someone to take the action mentioned.

It has the form: *have* + **direct object** + **past participle**

- An expression like *have something done* can be used to show that someone does the work for you, e.g.
  Ralph repaired his car = Ralph did the work.
  Ralph had his car repaired = Someone else did the work.

1 **It was found** to be empty.
   It is thought to be missing.
   It is believed to be true.
   It was understood that he would do it.

2 **It is reported** that over a hundred people died in the
   explosion.
   It is said that his income is over £200 a minute.

3 How did that teapot **get broken**?
   He sat too near the fire and his sweater **got scorched**.
   Our cat **got run over** last week.
   Harriet **got lost** on the Underground.

4 We **had the garage door replaced**.
   She **is having her hair cut short**.
   They **did not have the carpet cleaned**.

Finite and Non-finite Verbs

In each sentence there is normally at least one verb that has both a **subject** and a **tense**. This is called a **finite** verb (→ 1). Some parts of a verb are **non-finite**. The **present** and **past participles** and the *to infinitive* are the most common of these. The base form is often used in a non-finite way. Every verb can be used in a clause in either a **finite** or **non-finite** way.

• A verb is finite if it is found in a clause in combination with a subject and a tense (→ 2).

• It is non-finite if it is used:

– without the verb having a tense (→ 3), or
– with no agreement between the subject (if there is one) and the verb (→ 4).

A compound verb is actually made up of one finite part, which is always the first auxiliary verb, while the remaining non-finite parts are the base form or the participles (→ 5). For convenience, however, we normally regard the entire verb phrase as finite.

The Simple Present and Simple Past forms of a verb are always finite (→ 6).

• A non-finite verb is sometimes used immediately after a finite verb (→ 7). Often a noun or pronoun can come between the finite verb and the non-finite one (→ 8). See p. 116 and p. 118 for the more on this.

• When the second verb is an *-ing* form coming after a noun or pronoun, there can be a difference in grammar between two similar sentences. Both sentences in example 9 are acceptable, although the first example might seem ambiguous to some people. In the second sentence, the *-ing* form is used as a verbal noun (→ 9). See also p. 144.

1 **We want** Charlie to act as club secretary.
   I like to take photographs of insects.
   Coming home last night **I saw** a huge moth on a
   streetlamp.

2 **I walked** home.
   We saw a huge moth.
   They appreciate a little praise now and then.

3 **To open**, tear off the tab.
   Looking around, he noticed a letter on the floor.
   Fatigued by the heat, they stopped for a drink.

4 **That plan failing**, he gave up.
   Our guests departed, we felt a little depressed.

5 *The finite part of the verb phrase is in bold:*

   I **may** *have been joking* when I **said** that.
   Hetty **was** *running* around in circles.
   I **had** *been living* in a dream for months.
   Outi **is** *coming* home at 6 o'clock this evening.

6 I **sing**.   We **tell** stories at night.
   Maya **laughed**.   The shelter **collapsed**.

7 *A finite verb phrase is followed by a non-finite verb*
   phrase:

   I **like** *to take* photographs of insects.
   Harriet really **disliked** *washing* dirty dinner dishes.
   I certainly **wouldn't want** *to see* him again.
   We **persuaded** them *to join* us.

8 We **want** Charlie *to act* as club secretary.
   She **wanted** him *to clean* his hands in the bathroom.
   She **disliked** him *cleaning* his hands over the sink.

9 She disliked **him** cleaning his hands over the sink.
   She disliked **his** cleaning his hands over the sink.

The Non-finite Parts of the Verb

Non-finite parts of a verb are those that do not indicate number or person or tense. The common non-finite forms are:
– the **base form**,
– the **present participle** or *-ing* form,
– the **past participle**,
– the *to* **infinitive**.

There are also other non-finite forms, such as:
– the **progressive** *to* infinitive: *to be teaching*
– the **perfect** *to* infinitive: *to have taught*
– the **passive** *to* infinitive: *to be taught*

The Base Form

As well as serving as the verb form on which most of the other parts of the verb are based, the **base form** is frequently used as a non-finite part of the verb. Because of this it is sometimes called the '*bare infinitive*' or '*infinitive without to*'.

The **base form** is used as a **non-finite** part of the verb in these ways:
– after modal verbs (→ 1).
– after *let's* (suggestion) and *let* (permission) and *make* (compulsion) (→ 2).
– after *feel, hear, see, watch* + an **object** (→ 3).
– after a *to* infinitive to which it is joined by *and* (→ 4).
– after *would rather* and *had better* (→ 5).

Verbs of perception may be followed either by the **base form** or by the *-ing* form. There is often a change of sentence meaning (→ 6).
These verbs include: *see, hear, feel, smell, listen to, watch.*

1 You must **stop** at the kerb before you cross.
   He should **think** before he speaks.

2 **Let's invite** Annette to a late supper!
   Let *the cat* **go**!
   Make *Peter* **stop** it!
   Let *him* **finish** what he was saying!

3 I heard *him* **run** downstairs and later we saw *them*
   leave the house.

4 I want you to sit and **listen** carefully.
   They had to wait and **see**.

5 We would rather **go** out but we had better **stay** home
   and finish this painting.

6 We watched her **park** the car = *we watched the whole
   event.*
   We watched her **parking** the car = *we may only have
   seen part of the event.*
   I heard a cuckoo **call** = *I heard just one call.*
   We heard the birds **singing** = *We heard part of the
   song of the birds.*

The *to* Infinitive

The *to* infinitive is used as follows:
- after an adjective of quality such as *small, tall, agreeable, pleasant, funny* that is used in combination with *too* + adjective of quality (→ 1), or *not* + adjective of quality + *enough* (→ 2).
- after adjectives of emotion such as: *angry, happy, glad, sad, sorry, surprised*, to express the reason for the emotion (→ 3).
- after an adjective such as: *good, kind, nice, silly, wrong*, (sometimes + *of* + another **noun phrase**) (→ 4).
- after a **WH-** word such as: *how, what, where, whether, which, who, whom* (→ 5).
- after a noun phrase such as *a good idea, a good thing, a mistake* (sometimes + *for* + another **noun phrase**) (→ 6).
- after an adjective such as *easy, difficult, hard, impossible* + *for* + **noun phrase** (→ 7).
- after a verb followed by *for*, e.g. *ask, wait* + *for* + **noun phrase** (→ 8).

- Sometimes the particle *to* can be used without the verb, provided the meaning is clear. This is usually the case when the whole verb form is used in a previous sentence or clause (→ 9).

- The *to* infinitive can be used to express purpose or necessity after a verb followed by a pronoun or a noun.
  Purpose: I brought *it* **to read** on the train = so that I could read it.
  Necessity: There is *work* **to do**! = work that must be done.

1 The child was **too small to reach** the switch.
   The knife was **too blunt to cut** the string.

2 The child was **not tall enough to reach** the switch.
   The knife was **not sharp enough to cut** the string.

3 I'm **glad to see** you but **sorry to hear** your news.

4 It was **good** *of you* **to come** and **kind** *of Jane* **to
   have sent** those flowers.
   It was **silly** *of Brian* **to go**.
   It was **kind** *of you* **to ring** me.

5 We have no idea **what to get** for Tim's birthday.
   I don't know **where to go**.
   I can't think **how to do it**.
   They were wondering **who to see** first.

6 It was **a mistake** *for Jim* **to buy** that motorbike.
   It was **a good idea to stop** here.

7 It has never been **easy** *for David* **to sit** exams.

8 They **are waiting** *for us* **to decide**.

9 Did you **meet** Tina? I expected **to**, but I wasn't able **to**.
   Are you going to **visit** the museum? Yes, we hope **to**.

The *to* Infinitive and the *-ing* Form

The *to* infinitive and the *-ing* form (the present participle) can each be used after certain verbs.

Verbs followed by the *to* infinitive ($\rightarrow 1$) include: *agree, arrange, attempt, choose, decide, fail, hope, learn, manage, offer, plan, seem.*

Verbs followed by an **object + the *to* infinitive** ($\rightarrow 2$) include: *advise, allow, command, forbid, force, invite, order, persuade, remind, teach, tell.*

Verbs followed either directly by the **to infinitive** or by an **object + the *to* infinitive** ($\rightarrow 3$), ($\rightarrow 4$) include: *ask, expect, help, intend, like, love, hate, mean, prefer, want, wish.*

Verbs followed by the *-ing* form ($\rightarrow 5$) include: *avoid, be used to, delay, dislike, escape, finish, forgive, give up, go on, imagine.*

- Some verbs may be followed either by the *to* infinitive or by the *-ing* form with no change in meaning ($\rightarrow 6$).
  These verbs include: *begin, start, cease, continue, intend, like, love, hate, prefer.*

- Some verbs may be followed either by the *to* infinitive or by the *-ing* form but the meaning of the sentence changes depending on the form that is used.
  These verbs include: *try, forget, remember.*

Use of the verb followed by the *to* infinitive concentrates on the action. The action in both verbs is equally important ($\rightarrow 7$). Particularly after verbs such as *go* and *come* the *to* infinitive is understood to express purpose ($\rightarrow 8$).

Use of the verb followed by the *-ing* form concentrates on what happens. The second verb is really the object of the first one ($\rightarrow 9$). These verbs include: *remember, forget, try.* Some **set expressions** (idioms) are followed by *-ing*. These include: *it's not worth,* and *it's no fun* ($\rightarrow 10$).

1 I **agreed to help** Shona with her homework.
   The driver **attempted to remove** the flat tyre.
   I **hope to see** you again at the next meeting.

2 Peter advised Ron **to call the police.**
   Esther reminded her teacher **to set some revision**.

3 I certainly intended **to go** to the party.
   We really expected **Sally to pass** the exam.

4 Note this difference:
   I want **to have** a cat = *It will be my cat.*
   I want *her* **to have** a cat = *It will be her cat.*
   Dad likes **to wash** the car = *Dad washes the car.*
   Dad likes *John* **to wash** the car = *John washes the car.*

5 I usually **avoid going** into town late at night.
   Miriam **disliked peeling** potatoes.
   Have you **finished reading** *The Go Between*?

6 He began **to run**.   He began **running**.
   She likes **to swim**.   She likes **swimming**.
   I can't bear **to see** violence.
   I can't bear **seeing** violence.

7 We **forgot to pay** the milkman, so he left no milk.
   Has she **tried to use** a paint pad? It needs practice.

8 She has **gone to do** the shopping.
   They **came** to Brighton **to learn** English.

9 He **forgot** *paying the milkman* and paid him again.
   Has she **tried** *using a paint pad*? They're very good.

10 It's **no fun going** out alone.
   It's **no use phoning** him, he's gone away.
   It's **worth trying** one more time.

The Noun Phrase

A noun phrase is a word or group of words that can function as the **subject**, the **object**, or the **complement** in a sentence ($\rightarrow$ 1). See pp. 10-12 and pp. 202-204 for more information about these functions.
A noun phrase must always contain a noun or a pronoun.

A noun phrase may consist of only one word. That word will be either a noun or a pronoun ($\rightarrow$ 2).
A noun phrase may consist of more than one word. One of these words, a noun or a pronoun, is the **headword**. The other words describe or modify the headword ($\rightarrow$ 3).

Words that go before the headword are called **premodifiers**.
A noun can be premodified by:
– a determiner ($\rightarrow$ 4). See p. 146.
– one or more adjectives ($\rightarrow$ 5). See pp. 166–170.
– a number, another noun, or the present participle or past participle of a verb ($\rightarrow$ 6).

Words that go after the headword are called **postmodifiers**.
A noun can be postmodified by:
– a prepositional phrase (a noun phrase with a preposition in front of it) ($\rightarrow$ 7).
– a subordinate clause (usually one beginning with a **WH–** word) ($\rightarrow$ 8). See p. 234.
– less commonly, certain adjectives ($\rightarrow$ 9). See p. 168.

● Personal pronouns are only rarely premodified or postmodified ($\rightarrow$ 10). See p. 168.

1 **The Area Manager** interviewed **all the applicants**
   on Tuesday.
   Lydia was **the successful applicant**.

2 **Mary** left late.   **She** left late.
   Cheese is expensive.   **It** is expensive.

3 the tall **girl**   the very tall **girl**
   a strikingly beautiful **girl**
   the tall **girl** with green eyes

4 **the** girl   **that** boy
   a spider   **some** rice

5 **tall** girls
   tall dark girls   **tall dark handsome** men

6 **three** days   the **railway station** buffet
   an **annoying** habit   a **worried** man

7 the person **in the corner**
   the view **above the trees**
   the house **opposite the church**
   the rocks **under the sea**

8 All the women **who had gathered there** finally went
   away.
   Milk **that has been kept too long** can go sour.

9 a battle **royal**
   the president **elect**

10 **silly** me
   poor old you
   we **who fought this campaign**
   you **with the red coat**

Types of Noun

Nouns can be classified according to what they refer to.

A. Nouns that are really names are called **proper nouns.**
Proper nouns usually refer to a particular, named person or
thing.

They include:
    the names of specific people ($\to$ 1).
    geographical items ($\to$ 2).
    days of the week, months, and annual Church
    festivals ($\to$ 3).
    patented goods and trade names ($\to$ 4).
    newspaper and magazine titles ($\to$ 5).
    shop, cinema, theatre names, buildings ($\to$ 6).

Titles are the polite or professional labels that we give to
people ($\to$ 7). A person's title is usually placed before his or
her name.
Proper nouns and titles are always written to start with a
capital letter.

B. All the other nouns that refer to things or species are
called **common nouns** ($\to$ 8).

• A common noun enables us to refer to something or
  someone as a member of the set of similar things. For
  example *a cat* is a member of the set of all cats.

Common nouns can be divided into the following groups,
according to their meaning:
Abstract nouns. These refer to intangible items ($\to$ 9).
Concrete nouns. These refer to tangible items ($\to$ 10). A
concrete noun may refer to a living thing (**animate** nouns)
or a physical object (**inanimate** nouns).
Collective nouns. These refer to collections of people or
animals ($\to$ 11).

Continued

1   Anna Dickinson   John Lennon
    Lucy White   Mrs Merton

2   Spain   Mt Everest
    China   England
    The Thames   Paris
    Covent Garden   Balcombe Road

3   Thursday   June
    Christmas   Easter

4   Hoover   Persil
    Jaguar   Honda Accord

5   The Times   House and Garden
    The New Scientist   Time Out

6   The Odeon   Next
    The Royal Mews   Abbey National

7   **Doctor** Johnson   **Sir** George Hardie.
    Professor James   **President** Clinton

8   I put the **sugar** in those **tea-cups** there.
    My **brother** and **sister** visited my **mother**.
    The **anger** that John felt was overwhelming.

9   honesty   anger
    idea   time
    ugliness   behaviour

10 pig   granite
    table   butcher
    brother and **sister**   the **sugar** in those **tea-cups**

11 a **herd** of cows   a **swarm** of bees

Types of Noun (ctd)

Nouns may also be classified according to the words with
which they are used, that is:
– whether or not the noun gives us information about
  singular and **plural number**.
– the other words that can be used in the same noun
  phrase.
This gives us a useful distinction between **count nouns**
and **uncountable nouns**.

Count nouns refer to things that we can count: *one cat,
two cats, seventeen cats,*and so on. They have singular and
plural forms, which are shown by the spelling. They must
be used with a determiner if they are singular (→ 1).

Uncountable nouns refer to:
– things that are not normally thought of as countable (→ 2).
– qualities or abstract ideas (→ 3).
Uncountable nouns do not usually have a plural form.
They are are followed by a singular verb. They are not
normally used with the indefinite article. You cannot talk
about '*an advice*' or '*a money*'. When it is necessary to
think of an item as countable it has to be used with a
partitive noun (→ 4). See p. 126.

Some examples of the commonest uncountable nouns are:
*advice, anger, beauty, behaviour, conduct, despair,
evidence, furniture, happiness, homework, information,
safety, knowledge, leisure, money, news, progress, research,
jumble.*

• Verbal nouns (p. 144), which are formed from the
  present participle of verbs, can also be used as
  uncountable nouns (→ 5).

• Note that nouns that are uncountable in English may
  be count nouns in other languages. See p. 128.

Continued

1   **Dog**s ran wild in the streets.
    The dog is loose again.
    Fetch **a chair** for Maddy, will you, Leonie?
    We have bought **six new dining chairs**.

2   John asked me for **advice** about new **furniture**.
    The news is bad again.
    Anna gave us further **information** about her **work**.
    Homework occupied much of Sonia's evening.

3   **Knowledge** about outer **space** is increasing daily.
    Trevor gave **evidence** about Paul's **unhappiness**.
    Anger is one of the seven deadly sins.

4   He bought **seven sheets of** hardboard.
    I was grateful for **all** your recent helpfulness.

5   Why don't you try **walking** as an exercise?
    Brian was told to stop **smoking**.
    The **ringing** in his ears continued.

Types of Noun (ctd)

Mass nouns

These are nouns that refer to a substance that can be
divided or measured but not counted, e.g. *sugar, water*.
They do not usually have an indefinite article in front (→ 1).
Mass nouns only take a plural in special cases.
They can be counted when they refer to:
– a particular type or types of the substance (→ 2).
– a certain measure of the substance (→ 3).

• Mass nouns are often used together with a partitive
  noun (→ 4).

Partitive nouns

Partitive nouns are commonly followed by *of*.
They are used when we need to talk about a part of a mass
noun or when we need to count the quantity of something
that is referred to by an uncountable noun or a mass noun,
especially when it is necessary to talk about:
– measurements and quantities with mass nouns (→ 5).
– individual items with uncountable nouns (→ 6).
– a collection of count nouns (→ 7).

• Many collective nouns can be used as partitive nouns.
  See p. 122.

Continued

1 **Meat** is usually more expensive than **cheese**.
Sugar is quite cheap.

2 **Many cold meats** are too expensive for me to buy.
Some French cheeses are exported.
The principal sugars are glucose, sucrose, and fruc-
tose.

3 **Two teas**, please.
He went up to the bar and ordered **two lagers**.

4 There are only **two pieces of furniture** in the room.
There are **three portions of meat** in this special
pack.
Five pints of lager, please.

5 three **pieces** of toast   a **slice** of cheese
a **bit** of fluff   two **spoonfuls** of sugar

6 Two **pieces** of furniture needed major repairs.
We needed several **lengths** of string.
There wasn't a **stick** of furniture in the whole house.

7 A dog can soon upset a **flock** of sheep.
He has bought a new **herd** of dairy cows.
a **crowd** of football supporters
All I saw was a **couple** of cats fighting.

Types of Noun (ctd)

Nouns that have both count and uncountable uses.
Most nouns are either count nouns or uncountable nouns,
as explained on p. 124. Some nouns, however, behave like
count nouns in some sentences and uncountable nouns in
other sentences. They usually have different meanings
depending on how they are used. For example *time, light,
history, space, laugh,* and *grocery* have more than one
meaning ($\rightarrow$ 1).

Some nouns that are count nouns in other languages are
normally used only in the singular form in English,
e.g. *information, advice* ($\rightarrow$ 2).

Some nouns are used only in the plural form even when
we are talking about one item, e.g. *trousers, clothes, jeans*
We have to use a partitive noun with *of* when referring to
a single item ($\rightarrow$ 3).

1 **Time** passed slowly.
   She did it four **times.**
   Light travels faster than sound.
   The **lights** in this room are too bright.
   History teaches us little, I'm afraid.
   The doctor will need to examine all the case **histories**.
   They went out into empty **space**.
   There are plenty of empty **spaces** on the shelves.
   If you work in a **grocery** you spend your life filling
   shelves with **groceries.**

2 He received all the necessary **information**.
   I don't need your **help**.

3 These **trousers** need cleaning.
   Put the **scissors** back when you have finished with
   them.
   He took up *a pair of* pliers.
   Elisabeth gathered up *a bundle of* clothes.

Gender of Nouns

In some languages nouns have **gender**, which means that a noun causes other words such as adjectives to change their spelling according to certain rules. Grammatical gender has little to do with biological gender. English does not have **grammatical gender** for nouns.

On the other hand, the **biological gender** of the thing or person referred to does affect a few areas of English grammar (→ 1). Gender distinctions are relevant where personal pronouns (p. 182) and possessive determiners (p. 154) have to be decided on. These distinctions are only noticeable in **singular** nouns (→ 2).

There are also special cases, such as the association of neuter gender with babies and small animals, or feminine gender with a vehicle (→ 3).

Nouns denoting male persons and animals are **masculine** in that they are used with the pronouns and possessive determiners *he, him, his* (→ 3).

Nouns denoting female persons and animals are **feminine** in that they used with the pronouns and possessive determiners *she, her, hers* (→ 4).

The pronouns and possessive determiners used to refer to common or **neuter** nouns are: *it, its* (→ 5). Nouns denoting inanimate objects and abstract notions are also neuter.

• Some nouns denoting people have the same form for masculine and feminine. Nouns used for a group, e.g. *government* or *team*, have **common** or **neuter** gender, even when we know that the group is made up exclusively of male or female members (→ 6).

Continued

1 a cow… **she** or **it**   a bull… **he** or **it**
   a girl… **she**   a boy… **he**

2 The **man** found **his** book.
   He had been looking for **it**.
   The **woman** found **her** book.
   She had been looking for **it**.

3 a mouse … **it**   a hen… **it**
   The **spider** spun **its web**.
   The **beetle** crawled into **its hole**.
   The **baby** threw down **its** rattle.
   I love my car because **she's** a marvellous runner.

4 Barry saw Linda. **He** called out to **her** that **he** had
   found **her** book.
   Marcia saw Paul. **She** called out to **him** that **she** had
   found **his** book.
   Madeleine saw Kim. **She** said 'Hello' to **her**.

5 a chair… **it**   a dog… **it**
   honesty… **it**   a tiger… **it**
   The **truth** will emerge. **It** always does.

6 The **government** has changed **its** policy.
   The **government** have changed **their** policy.
   The **team** won **its / their** match.

Gender of Nouns (ctd)

With some nouns of common gender it might be possible to specify the gender if we had sufficient information. But if we do not have this knowledge, the choice of pronoun or possessive determiner becomes a problem ($\to$ 1).

In informal and spoken English, ***their*** is sometimes used after a singular noun or an indefinite pronoun. See p. 192. Many people consider this grammatically unacceptable, but it is widely used to avoid repetitions of *his or her* or *him or her*, where the gender really does not matter ($\to$ 2).

The specialized terms used to name male, female and neutered animals show a number of gender differences ($\to$ 3). Gender differences are also shown in the nouns that indicate relationships ($\to$ 4).

- Many nouns denoting an occupation have common gender ($\to$ 5).

- Some nouns have related forms for masculine and feminine. These forms are often marked by suffixes such as *-er* or *-ess* ($\to$ 3), ($\to$ 4).

Some occupations and professions have a special feminine form for the noun ($\to$ 6). Many people prefer to avoid these forms, regarding the distinction as unnecessary ($\to$ 7). Some speakers prefer to use a different form of the word or an entirely different word in order to avoid a gender-marked noun ($\to$ 8). If necessary, the gender of a common noun can be made clear by adding a descriptive term such as *woman* or *male / female* ($\to$ 9).

- If we are discussing a country from an emotional, economic, or political viewpoint we sometimes use feminine gender ($\to$ 10).

1   a driver…he / she
    the cook…he / she
    doctor…he / she

2   Each **student** must apply to **his or her** tutor for an
    extension.
    Everyone must apply to **their** tutor for an extension.
    Someone has left **their** coat in my room.

3 | horse | mare | stallion | gelding |
    |-------|------|----------|---------|
    | – | cow | bull | steer |
    | sheep | ewe | ram | – |

4 | parent | mother | father |
    |----------|----------|--------|
    | child | daughter | son |
    | waitress | waiter | |
    | heroine | hero | |

5 | engineer | doctor | programmer |
    |----------|--------|------------|
    | mechanic | lawyer | driver |

6   Call on your bank **manager** today.
    Sue was **manageress** of the salon.
    The life of a **shepherd** is difficult even in these days.
    Barbara dressed up as a **shepherdess** for the play.

7   Marianne Moore is a very interesting **poet**.
    Judi Dench is one of our finest **actors**.
    Mrs Jones has been promoted to Branch **Manager**.

8   the chair**man**   the chair**person**   the **chair**

9   Would you prefer to see **a woman doctor**?
    Male staff should use locker room B.

10 **Spain** is a major car manufacturer. **She** exports cars
    to the UK.

Case of Nouns

Case is the way in which a noun can be given a change of spelling (an **inflection**), which indicates that the noun has a particular function in a clause. English nouns have two **cases.** (See also p. 182 for personal pronouns, which can have three cases.)

A. The **basic** case. The form of the noun does not change. (The plural form is number, not case). The noun can be the **subject** or **object** in a clause or the **object** of a preposition (→ 1).

B. The **possessive** case (sometimes called the **genitive**). The noun does change. It has two forms:
- the *-'s possessive* (a singular inflected form) (→ 2).
- the *-s' possessive* (an inflected form in the plural) (→ 3).

There is also the *of possessive* (a phrase with *of* followed by a noun) (→ 4). The *of possessive* is not just a different way of saying the same thing as the *-'s possessive* (→ 5). The *-'s possessive* is generally used only with nouns referring to animate items and in time phrases (→ 6). The *of possessive* is generally used with nouns referring to inanimate things and abstract ideas (→ 7).

The function of the possessive case in English is to:
- show possession (→ 8).
- show a relationship, with a person as either as the originator, or the user of the thing named (→ 9).
- indicate that a place is where someone works or lives (→ 10).
- show that something is a part of a whole (→ 11).
- add a descriptive element which premodifies a headword (→ 12). It is a type of determiner. See also p. 146.

Continued

1 The **man** was mending his **car**.
  The **car** was being mended by a **man**.

2 *one dog*   *one boy*
  the **dog's** bones   the **boy's** books

3 *more than one dog*   *more than one boy*
  the **dogs'** bones   the **boys'** books

4 the side **of the ship**   the end **of the queue**

5 the **boy's** pencil   ***but not*** *the pencil of the boy*

6 the **driver's** foot   the **dog's** nose
  today's newspaper   a **week's** holiday

7 the leg **of the table**   the arm **of the sofa**
  the wheel **of the car**   the foot **of the bed**
  the world **of ideas**   the power **of thought**

8 the **boy's** books   the **dog's** blanket

9 her **parents'** consent   the **student's** letter
  a **women's** club   the **children's** park

10 a **grocer's**   the **butcher's**
  a **solicitor's**   my **aunt's**

11 the leg **of the table**   the **dog's** nose
  the wheel **of the car**   the **girl's** shoulder

12 **writer's** cramp   **Devil's** Dyke
  A **Winter's** Tale   **plumber's** mate

Case of Nouns (ctd)

Rules for the -'s (apostrophe -s) and -s' (-s apostrophe)
possessive formation are as follows:
- most singular nouns add an apostrophe + s ($\rightarrow$ 1).
- most plural nouns add an apostrophe after the plural
  form -s ($\rightarrow$ 2).

There are exceptions for the following:
- common nouns that end in -s in the singular. When these
  are made plural the choice of -'s or -s' is optional ($\rightarrow$ 3).
- plural nouns not ending in -s, for example those that
  that have a plural ending in -en. These add an
  apostrophe + s ($\rightarrow$ 4).
- proper nouns and common nouns that end in -s. These
  usually add -'s in the singular unless the final sound of
  the basic word is [-iz] ($\rightarrow$ 5).

Compound nouns (See p. 138) put the -'s or the -s' at the
end of the complete compound ($\rightarrow$ 6).

Noun phrases that are descriptive of someone's role or
profession put the -'s on the headword of the phrase ($\rightarrow$ 7).
If they use an *of* construction the -'s or -s' usually goes on
the last noun ($\rightarrow$ 8).

1   a **girl's** ring   a **cat's** face

2   the **boys'** football   five young **girls'** faces

3   a cactus   the **cactus'** spines
                                     the **cactus's** habitat

4   **children's**   **men's**

5   Mrs **Evans's** car   Mr **Jones's** fence
     Keats's poetry   the **Bates's** cat
     I like **Dickens's** novels
     Peter **Bridges'** car

6   my mother-in-law   my **mother-in-law's** car
     the runner-up   the **runner-up's** deposit
     the fire-fighters   the **fire-fighters'** efforts

7   **a stock market analyst's** annual income
     the senior hospital consultant's weekly visit

8   **the President of Austria's** official car
     the director of marketing's personal assistant

Compound Nouns

A compound noun is one formed from two or more other
words. The meaning of the whole compound is often
different from the meaning of the two words on their own.
Compound nouns are very common. The main noun is
normally the last one (→ 1).

Compound nouns are commonly formed from the
following word combinations (→ 2):
– a noun + a noun,
– a verb + a noun,
– an adjective + a noun,
– a phrasal verb used as a noun,
– a particle + a noun.

• The term **particle** is used for a word which could be
either an adverb or a preposition.

Compound nouns can be written:
– as one word (→ 3).
– as two words (→ 4).
– with a hyphen (→ 5).

Consult a dictionary to discover how the word is normally
written. There are often alternative forms to be found,
e.g. *girl friend, girl-friend,* and *girlfriend* are all currently
acceptable forms of the same compound noun.

Nouns as modifiers

The compound noun *girlfriend* names a special sort of
friend. Nouns can also be used as **modifiers** without
forming a compound noun (→ 6). A noun that is used as a
modifier has the same function as an adjective. The first
noun usually makes the second one more specific, but we
do not think of it as part of a combination that forms a
new word. See p. 168 for more on modifiers.

1 teapot
   washing **machine**
   self-**control**

   head**ache**
   driving **licence**
   record-**changer**

2 *a noun + a noun:*
   a verb + a noun:
   an adjective + a noun:
   a phrasal verb:
   a particle + a noun:

   boyfriend
   breakfast
   software
   a break-in
   overseer

   skinhead
   flashlight
   hardware
   a let-out
   aftershave

3 bookcase
   birdcage

   wallpaper
   snowflake

4 post office
   eye shadow

   fire engine
   cough drops

5 window-cleaner
   lamp-post

   air-conditioning
   fish-hook

6 a **concrete** slab
   a **car** mechanic

   old **oak** beams
   a **brewery** manager

Number in Nouns

Singular number is used when the noun refers to one item. **Plural number** is used when the noun refers to more than one item.

Count nouns have both singular and plural forms.

Uncountable nouns and **mass nouns** do not normally have a plural form. See p. 122 for more on the types of noun.

The regular plural ending of an English noun is *-s* ($\rightarrow$ 1).

These are the exceptions to the normal pattern:

Singular noun ending	*Plural noun ending*	
-s, -ss, -ch, -x, -zz	-es	($\rightarrow$ 2).
-o	-s or -es	($\rightarrow$ 3).
consonant + y	-ies	($\rightarrow$ 4).
vowel + y	-s	($\rightarrow$ 5).
-f	-s or -ves	($\rightarrow$ 6).
-fe	-ves	($\rightarrow$ 7).

Irregular plurals

Some nouns have two plural forms ($\rightarrow$ 8).
Some of them the same form in the singular and plural ($\rightarrow$ 9).
A few change a vowel to form the plural ($\rightarrow$ 10).
Many of these are words used to denote animals.

Some nouns form the plural in *-en* ($\rightarrow$ 11).

- The word *brethren* is an alternative plural for *brother* but has the special sense of 'members of a religious group'.

Continued

Since it is not possible to give more than a selection of the irregular forms, you should check in a dictionary if you are in doubt. If the dictionary does not show the plural form, then you can assume that it is regular.

1	cat	cats

2	focus	focuses
	princess	princesses
	church	churches
	box	boxes
	buzz	buzzes

3	hero	heroes
	piano	pianos
	potato	potatoes

4	baby	babies
	hobby	hobbies

5	key	keys
	ray	rays

6	hoof	hoofs *or* hooves
	dwarf	dwarfs *or* dwarves
	thief	thieves
	roof	roofs

7	knife	knives
	life	lives

8	fish	fish *or* fishes

9	a sheep	ten sheep
	a deer	seven deer

10	man	men	woman women
	foot	feet	mouse mice

11	child	children	ox oxen

Number in Nouns (ctd)

Compound nouns normally form the plural by adding -s to the last word of the compound (→ 1). There are a few exceptions.

A compound noun formed from a verb and an adverb adds -s to the last word (→ 2), but a compound noun formed from a noun and an adverb makes the first word plural (→ 3).

Compound nouns with *man* or *woman* as the first word make both words plural (→ 4).

A compound word which ends in *-ful* normally adds *-s* after *-ful*, but there is an alternative form with the *-s* following the base noun (→ 5).

Plural nouns with singular reference

Some nouns referring to clothes and tools where two equal parts are joined together, e.g. *trousers, binoculars,* and *tongs,* are treated as being plural and are followed by a verb in the plural (→ 6). To talk about one of these items we use the expression *a pair of...*(→ 7). To talk about more than one we talk about however many *pairs of...*(→ 8).

• When used as ordinary numbers, words such as *dozen* and *million* have no plural form (→ 9). When used to mean an indefinitely large number, they do have a plural form, which can be used as a partitive (→ 10).

Foreign plurals

Nouns that have come into English from foreign languages can:

– keep the plural form of the language they come from (→ 11).

– have plurals formed according to the rules for plural in English in preference to the foreign plurals (→ 12).

– have two plurals: one from the foreign language and the other formed according to the rules for plural formation in English. The foreign plural is usually kept for scientific or specialized use (→ 13).

1   a girl friend   three girl friends
    a bookcase   two bookcases

2   an Indian take-away   two Indian **take-aways**

3   a passer-by   several **passers-by**

4   a manservant   five men**servants**
    a woman doctor   several **women** doctors

5   a cupful   three **cupfuls / cupsful**
    a spoonful   two **spoonfuls / spoonsful**

6   My shorts **are** torn.
    The scissors **are** on the table.

7   John bought **a pair of jeans**.

8   Martina bought **five pairs of tights.**

9   **nine million** stars   **two dozen** glasses

10 There are **millions** of pebbles on the beach.
    I saw **dozens** of children in the playground.

11 an axis   two axes
    a crisis   two crises

12 a memorandum   several memorandums
                                  (*instead of* memoranda).

13 an index   indexes / indices
    a formula   some formulas / formulae

Verbal Nouns

The **verbal noun** is the *-ing* form, i.e. the present participle of the verb, used as a noun (→ 1). It can be used in all the places that a noun can be used, but still keeps some characteristics of the verb. It is sometimes called the **gerund**.

The verbal noun normally functions as an uncountable noun (→ 1). However, there are some uses of the verbal noun that can be preceded by an indefinite article or used in the plural (→ 2).

The verbal noun can be preceded by the definite article, by adjectives, and by possessives (→ 3).

Just like any noun, the verbal noun can function:
– as a **subject** (→ 4).
– as the **complement** of the verb *be* (→ 5).
– as an **object** after certain verbs (→ 6). See also p. 112.
– after **prepositions** to make a prepositional phrase (→ 7).

Verbal nouns are also used:
– after some phrasal verbs such as: *be for / against, give up, keep on, look forward to, put off* (→ 8).
– after certain set expressions such as: *can't stand, can't help, it's no use / good* (→ 9).

The **possessive determiner** is normally used with the verbal noun, especially in formal English. The direct object form of the personal pronoun is often used in informal speech (→ 10).

• The verbal noun also has:
– a perfect form: ***having ...ed*** (→ 11).
– a passive form: ***being ...ed*** (→ 12).
– a perfect passive form: ***having been ...ed*** (→ 13).

1 The **screaming** of the brakes terrified me.
   Smoking is prohibited.

2 He gave **a reading** from his latest volume of poetry.
   The **takings** were down this week in the shop.

3 Her marvellous **singing** won Helen the scholarship.

4 **Driving** was impossible.

5 Seeing is **believing**.
   His greatest pleasure is **working**.

6 Louisa likes **swimming** but Helen prefers **diving**.

7 Can you watch them **without laughing**?

8 She was all for **leaving** immediately.
   Linda gave up **swimming** but she kept on **dieting**.
   They were looking forward to **writing** home.

9 I can't stand **waiting** around.
   I can't help **getting** cross.
   It's no use **crying** over spilt milk.

10 Anna left the house without **my knowing**.
    Anna left the house without **me knowing**.

11 Martin was accused of **having cheated**.

12 **Being asked** did not bother me.

13 The car showed no sign of **having been touched**.

Determiners

Determiners are words that make the reference of nouns more specific.
If I write or say the word *'car'* I am only telling you that the thing is not, for example, a *'bicycle'*. When I say *'this car'* it becomes clear that I mean a particular car which is near me. If I change it to *'my car'* I am saying something quite specific about ownership.

Determiners can be divided into several kinds according to:
— their meaning
— what they may go with and where they may come in the noun phrase.

There are eight classes of determiners:
— the indefinite article *a* or *an* (→ 1). See p. 148.
— the definite article *the* (→ 2). See p. 150.
— the demonstratives *this, that, these, those* (→ 3). See p. 154.
— the possessives *my, your, his, her, its, our, their* (→ 4). See p. 154.
— the quantifiers *some, any, enough, no, all, both, half, double, several, much, many, more, most, few, fewer, fewest, a few, little* (meaning not much), *less, least, a little* (→ 5) See pp. 156-159.
— the numbers, cardinal (*one, two, three...*), and ordinal (*first, second, third...*) (→ 6). See p. 160.
— the distributives *each, every, either, neither* (→ 7) See p. 162.
— the exclamatives *what, such* (→ 8). See p. 162.

Generally, a noun phrase has only one determiner in it, or none at all. See p. 152. A few determiners, e.g. *all, both*, and the numbers, can be used together with another determiner. See p. 164.

Continued

1   A man was seen to push **an** old lady.
    An honest man would return the car to the owner.

2   **The** man chased **the** cat.

3   **This** book is better than **that** one.
    These apples are redder than **those** ones.

4   I gave **my** share to **her** sister.
    Shirley found **his** book in **her** car.

5   I have got **some** coffee but I haven't **any** sugar.
    Have you got **much** sugar?
    There were **no** dogs to be seen anywhere.
    Both girls saw the accident.
    Few people know the answer to your problem.
    The teacher gave **little** help with the problem.

6   The **one** thing I ask of you is silence.
    My **two** brothers are lawyers.
    Three men were found hiding in the building.
    The **second** girl was Sue.
    At the **third** stroke it will be 9.45 precisely.

7   **Each** child is given his or her own book.
    Every girl was given a number to wear.
    Either book will help you with the problem.

8   **What** nonsense!
    What a shame!
    Such a fuss over a small thing!

The Indefinite Article

The indefinite article is *a* or *an*. The form *an* is used before a word that starts with a vowel sound (→ 1).

The indefinite article is used with singular count nouns:
- to refer to a person or a thing that you are mentioning for the first time in a conversation or a piece of writing (→ 2).
- to refer to a person or a thing about which you do not want to be specific (→ 3).
- to refer to a person or a thing about which you cannot be more specific because there is not enough information (→ 4).
- in definitions (→ 5).
- when you refer to a person's profession (→ 6).
- to express a quantity, unless there is a contrast involved, when *one* must be used (→ 7). The equivalent for plural nouns is *some* or no determiner at all. See p. 152.

It is the sound, not the spelling, that decides where *an* is used. For example, although *unique* begins with a vowel, the sound at the beginning resembles a y- sound (→ 8). You would not use *an* before *unique*. There are a few words that begin with a silent *h-*, in front of which *an* should be used. They are: *heir, heiress, honest, honour, hour*.

- Very formal or old-fashioned speakers also use the *an* form with some words beginning with an *h-* that is not silent, especially *historical* and *hotel* (→ 9).

Continued

1 **a** girl   **a** cat
   an unbearable girl   **an** engineer

2 **A** man was seen driving away **a** black car.

3 I stopped off at **a** shop to buy **a** newspaper.
   You pass **a** petrol station just before you get to our
   turning.

4 **A** man called to see you this afternoon.
   There was **a** telephone call for you a minute ago.

5 **An** octopus is **a** sea creature with eight tentacles.

6 Her father is **a** dentist and her mother is **a** teacher.

7 I want **a** needle and **a** thimble.
   I had only **a** glass of wine.
   There is **one** glass of wine left in the bottle.
   Guy has bought **a** sailboard.
   Seven racing yachts and **one** sailboard left the landing.

8 **an** idiot   **an** awful mistake
   a unicorn   **a** unique experience

9 I wajted **an** hour.
   They joined **a** historical society.
   They joined **an** historical society. *(old-fashioned
   English)*
   They were staying at **a** hotel.
   They were staying at **an** hotel. *(old-fashioned English)*

The Definite Article

The definite article is **the**.

The definite article is used with singular and plural nouns.
It is used both with count nouns and uncountable nouns:
–   to make definite or specific reference to a person or a
    thing that has already been referred to (→ 1).
–   to refer to a person or thing that is already specific
    because of what those talking already know (→ 2). In
    the first example, *'the children'* would be members of
    our family and *'the swimming pool'* is the swimming
    pool we normally go to.
–   when generalizing about a whole class or species,
    usually of plants or animals. A singular noun is used for
    this purpose (→ 3). The first example means
    'The elephant species is hunted.'
–   when followed by an adjective used as a noun indicating
    nationality or when generalizing about a whole class of
    people (→ 4). *The Dutch* in the first example means
    'Dutch people in general'.
–   before the names of rivers, groups of islands, seas,
    oceans, and mountain ranges (→ 5).
–   before the names of certain public institutions, most
    newspapers, and some magazines (→ 6).
–   before parts of the body when these are referred to in an
    impersonal way (→ 7).

•   The definite article is rarely used with titles. Proper
    nouns that refer to persons, such as *Sue* and *Ron,* and
    proper nouns used in conjunction with titles, such as
    Queen Elizabeth, Doctor Thomas, and *Captain Parry,*
    only take a definite article if:
–   they stand for the name of a place or thing (→ 8).
–   a distinction is being made between people who have
    identical names. This use can give emphasis to the noun
    (→ 9).

1 **A** man rounded the corner and looked·hard at a row of parked cars, buses, and lorries. **The** man then crossed the road in order to inspect **the** vehicles more closely.

2 Let's take **the** children to **the** swimming pool.
   Did you switch **the** heating on?
   There were drinks in **the** fridge but **the** beer was soon finished.

3 **The** elephant is, unfortunately, hunted for its tusks.
   The egg is a very versatile source of nourishment.

4 **The Dutch** are very skilful engineers.
   The poor were crowding the streets of the capital.
   The homeless were sheltered in the church.

5 **The** Thames   **The** Hebrides
   The North Sea   **The** Pacific

6 **The** British Museum   **The** Hilton Hotel
   The Lyceum Theatre   **The** Houses of Parliament
   The Independent   **The** Guardian
   The Listener   **The** New Scientist

7 A stone struck him on **the hand**.
   Martin hit him on **the head**.

8 **The Queen** is opening Parliament.
   Queen Elizabeth is opening Parliament.
   The Queen Mother has gone to the races.
   The Queen Elizabeth II is on a long cruise.
   We had a drink in **the Admiral Nelson**.

9 **The David Parry I know** is not the one you were talking about.
   The Mr Ross who called lives just along the street.
   Not *the* Larry Hagman?

Nouns used without a Determiner

Certain noun phrases do not have a determiner at all.
The omission of a determiner is always significant.

It is usual to omit the determiner when you use a noun or
noun phrase in the plural to make a generalization ($\rightarrow$ 1).

Singular nouns that are uncountable are used without a
determiner when you are making a general reference ($\rightarrow$ 2).

- This is particularly true when the uncountable noun is
  used for the first time in a general way in the course of
  a conversation or piece of writing. They can be used with
  a determiner when the reference becomes specific ($\rightarrow$ 3).
  For example, you can ask someone if they like *cake* as
  a rule, and then ask the person if she would like some
  of *your cake*.

There are a number of idiomatic expressions that usually
omit a determiner. Examples are expressions that refer to:
- travel, when you proceed *by*: bicycle, car, bus, train,
  ship, boat, plane ($\rightarrow$ 4).
- time with the prepositions *at, before,* or *by*, dawn,
  sunrise, sunset, noon, midnight, night, supper, dinner,
  day, night, ($\rightarrow$ 5).
- meals: to have *breakfast, tea, lunch* ($\rightarrow$ 6).
- institutions, with the prepositions *to* or *in*: church,
  hospital, prison, school, work ($\rightarrow$ 7).
- seasons of the year, when you are generalizing, e.g:
  in spring, in summer, in autumn, in winter ($\rightarrow$ 8).

All of these words are used with the definite article,
however, when you are talking about a specific time, place,
season, etc. ($\rightarrow$ 9).

1 He sells **cars** for a living.
   Tigers are nearing extinction.
   Onions are good for you.
   Rolling grassy hills rise on all sides of the town.

2 New **information** is now available.
   Do you like **cake**?
   This shop sells **furniture.**

3 **The** information was accurate.
   Would you like some of **the** cake?.
   The old dog kept blundering into **the** furniture.

4 Anna went **by bicycle** but Lucy went **by car**.
   Philip left **by car** but most of his journey was **by
   plane**.
   Paul travelled **on foot** for many kilometres.

5 Catherine rose **at dawn** and went to bed **at sunset**.
   I work well **by day** but my sister prefers to work **by
   night**.

6 Jane had **breakfast** at home.
   She met Diana **for lunch.**

7 John went **to hospital** after he had been **to work**.
   Lucy has been kept late **in school** every day.
   Ruth was **at home** all day.

8 **In autumn**, apples and plums are ripe.
   Early mornings **in summer** are bright.

9 Philip travelled by **the same train** as Mehandra.
   Just look at **the wonderful sunset** this evening.
   We put the old tables in **the church**.
   I usually prune the trees **in the winter**.
   I can't work well **in the summer**.

Demonstratives

Demonstratives are used to specify the distance or placing of an item in relation to the speaker.

The **demonstratives** are: *this, that, these, those*.
This and *these* refer to objects near the speaker ($\rightarrow$ 1).
The reference may be nearness in time, especially future time ($\rightarrow$ 2).
That and *those* refer to objects that are further away from the speaker ($\rightarrow$ 3).
This and *that* are used before singular count nouns and uncountable nouns ($\rightarrow$ 4).
These and *those* are used before plural count nouns ($\rightarrow$ 5).

Possessives

Possessives are used to specify the ownership of an item or, if the noun refers to something animate, to specify a relationship ($\rightarrow$ 6). The form of the possessive changes according to the number and gender of the person or thing that possesses the item ($\rightarrow$ 7).

Person	Singular	Plural
1st	my	our
2nd	your	your
3rd (Masculine)	his	their
3rd (Feminine)	her	their
3rd (Neuter)	its	their

- Possessive determiners, which can go into a noun phrase, should be distinguished from possessive pronouns, which can stand alone. See p. 186.

Another sort of possessive is the **possessive phrase**. This acts just like a possessive word but is a noun or noun phrase ending in -'s or -s'. A possessive phrase acts as a possessive determiner, but may itself include one of the other determiners ($\rightarrow$ 8).

1 **This apple** looks ripe.
   These apples come from Australia.

2 I'll call round **this** afternoon.
   The Garden Festival ends **this** Thursday.
   This summer is the warmest since 1976.

3 **That boy** in the next room is making too much noise.
   Those apples on the sideboard come from Spain.

4 I can touch **this picture,** but **that picture** is too high
   for me to reach.
   This book is mine, but **that paper** is not.

5 I am peeling **these potatoes** to put in a pie.
   Those men on the other side of the road are waiting
   for a bus.

6 That is **my car**.
   Mr Smith was **my teacher** in the sixth form.

7 **His sister** and **his brothers** all came.
   Their aunt lives here but **their cousins** are in Bonn.
   Your shoes are under **your bed**.

8 **Robert's** mother   **Sally's** new job
   the **visitors'** washroom   the **residents'** dining room
   a good day's work   **my wife's** cousin Emily
   The Prime Minister's Press Secretary

Quantifiers

Quantifiers are used to indicate the amount or quantity of something referred to by a noun. They differ from numbers because they indicate an approximate amount rather than an exact amount. They can be grouped according to their use.

all, some, any, much, enough, no
- You can use *all*, *some*, *any*, or *enough*, before a plural count noun or an uncountable noun (→ 1). You can use *no* before a singular or a plural count noun or an uncountable noun (→ 2).
- *some, any, much,* and *enough* are used to refer to a part of the item (→ 3).
  all and *no* refer to the whole of the item (→ 4).
- *some* is used in positive declarative sentences (→ 5).
- *any* is used in negative declarative sentences (→ 6).

• In interrogative sentences (questions), *any* is used when there is no particular expectation about the answer; *some* is used when the answer is expected to be positive (→ 7).

• The use of *no* with *there is / are* is very common. When *no* is used with other verbs, it is more formal than *did not (didn't) have any* (→ 8).

half, double, both
- *half* can be used with count nouns and with uncountable nouns (→ 9).
- *double* is used with uncountable nouns (→ 10).
- *both* is used to define two things represented by a plural count noun (→ 11).

See p. 164 for more information about quantifiers when they are used with other determiners.

Continued

1 Brian had **some** chips and beans for tea.
Anna gave me **all** her money.
Peter never has **any** time to visit his sister.

2 There were **no** pictures of the party.
No information about these events has been released.

3 Would you like **some** ice cream?
We didn't have **much** success that day.
I have not seen **enough** evidence to convince me.
I could not find **any** fresh vegetables at the shop.

4 **All the milk** has been used.
There is **no milk** in the fridge.

5 I have bought **some** chocolate.
I saw **some** small birds on the lawn.

6 I didn't buy **any** chocolate.
I have not seen **any** birds in these woods.

7 Have you **any** fresh cabbages today?
Has Paul **any** information about the car crash?
Would you like **some** cake, Indira?

8 **There was no post** today.
Formal He had **no trouble** finding the station.
Informal He **didn't have any trouble** finding the station.

9 **Half the sugar** spilt on the floor.
Half the pigeons took off in a panicky flight.

10 I'll need **double the amount** of sugar that it says here.
They want **double the money** to work over Easter.

11 **Both men** were given another chance.
Both dogs had to be put down.

Quantifiers (ctd)

The following quantifiers are used to express **graded**
amounts of an item. 'Graded' means that the quantity
extends from a low point on a scale to a higher point ($\rightarrow$ 1), ($\rightarrow$ 2).

- *many, more, most* are used with graded quantities of
  plural count nouns ($\rightarrow$ 1).
- *much, more, most* are used with graded quantities of
  uncountable nouns ($\rightarrow$ 2).
- *few, fewer, fewest* are used with graded quantities of
  plural count nouns ($\rightarrow$ 3).
- *little, less, least* are used with graded quantities of
  uncountable nouns ($\rightarrow$ 4).

- *a few,* and *a little* are different from *few* and *little* on
  their own because they have a positive sense.
  few means 'not many' ($\rightarrow$ 3), but *a few* means 'several'
  ($\rightarrow$ 5). *Little* means 'not much' ($\rightarrow$ 6), but *a little* means
  'some' ($\rightarrow$ 7).

- *Few* and *little* are often used in a negative sense to
  suggest disappointment or pessimism, while *a few* and
  a little are used in a positive sense to suggest that
  things are better than they might have been.

1 Have you seen **many ants** today?
  Yes, I've seen **more ants** than usual.
  I think **most ants** are swarming at this time of year.

2 I didn't put **much petrol** in the car.
  I think we need **more petrol.**
  Much irritation can be caused by buses being late.
  Most information is misleading in one way or
  another.

3 **Few people** know the answer.
  The fewer delays we have today, the better.
  He has **the fewest pupils** in his class because he does
  very advanced work.

4 There is **little chance** of our getting an extra day's
  holiday this year.
  He had **less opportunity** to revise than Margit.
  This soap powder causes **less frothing** than the other
  brand.
  She can't stand **the least opposition** to her will.

5 **A few kind people** helped the injured man.
  A few delays are inevitable.

6 The students were given **little help** with the problem
  and failed to complete it.
  Little encouragement was given to me by my
  employer.

7 The students solved the problem when the teacher
  gave them **a little help.**
  Everyone needs **a little encouragement.**
  I would like **a little milk** in my tea, please.

Numbers

There are two common kinds of number.

Cardinal numbers are used in all forms of counting that involves a total (→ 1).

The other type of number is the **ordinal**, which is used to give the place of something in an ordered sequence (→ 2).

Ordinals are mostly formed by adding *-th* to a cardinal number (→ 4). Exceptions are the words *first, second*, and *third*, and combinations which contain them, such as *twenty-first*.

Cardinal numbers can be used at the beginning of a noun phrase, like determiners (→ 1), or on their own, like pronouns (→ 3). Ordinal numbers are often used right after the definite article or after a possessive (→ 2).

- The words *next, last,* and *another* can also be regarded grammatically as ordinal numbers (→ 5). The words *next* and *last* are sometimes called **postdeterminers**, since they come after the word ***the*** or a possessive (→ 6).

- An ordinal, especially *next, last,* and *another,* can be used together with a cardinal number in the same noun phrase (→ 7).

- To show that a cardinal number is only approximate, the word, *some* is often used before it (→ 8).

1 **one** chair   **two** chairs
   a hundred people   **ten thousand** pounds

2 **The first** horse home was disqualified.
   It is **his fifty-first** birthday in August.
   This is to mark **the one hundred and fiftieth** year
   since the settlement of the colony.

3 And then there were **three**.
   Four of them came towards us.
   The other **two** went to get help.

4 fourth   twentieth   hundredth
   fifth   forty-ninth   millionth
   sixth   eighty-sixth   thousandth
   nine hundred and ninety ninth

5 The **third** day it rained was also the **last** day of our
   holiday.
   The **next** horse was declared the winner.
   Oh no, not **another** birthday!

6 The **next** three finishers also get a prize.
   The **last** three finishers will be eliminated.
   My **next** favourite artist is Gauguin.

7 The **first five** runners back were given a special prize.
   There are **another six** entrants for the main event.

8 **Some two hundred** people gathered in the pouring
   rain.

Distributives

Distributives are determiners used to talk about how something is shared out or divided.

The distributives are *each, every, either*, and *neither*. They are used with a singular noun ($\rightarrow$ 1).
- *each* and *every* are not used with proper nouns.
- *each* is used to refer to separate persons or things in a group of two or more ($\rightarrow$ 2).
- *every* is used to refer to all the persons or things in a group of three or more ($\rightarrow$ 3).
- *every* can be used in front of ordinal numbers ($\rightarrow$ 4). *'Every fourth house'* means *the fourth house, the eighth house, the twelfth house*, and so on. In such phrases, it means every house that is a multiple of the ordinal used.
- *either* is used to refer to one of two people or things ($\rightarrow$ 5).
- *neither* is used to exclude both of two people or things that are being referred to ($\rightarrow$ 6).

Exclamatives

Exclamatives are used to introduce an exclamation of surprise, admiration, or a similar emotion.

The exclamatives are: *what, such*.
Exclamations introduced by one of these words consist either of:
- the exclamative in a noun phrase alone ($\rightarrow$ 7).
- the exclamative and its noun phrase in a complete clause ($\rightarrow$ 8). The exclamative *what* can be followed by the indefinite article or sometimes by the definite article.

1 **Each child** was given a balloon.
   Every person at the fair was given a paper hat.
   Either child could win the prize.
   Neither plan will be successful.

2 Four girls came and **each one** sang a song.
   Each ticket should have a number.

3 **Every fisherman** has a boat.
   Twenty people came and she spoke to **every one**.

4 **Every third man** was dressed in black.
   In this street **every fourth house** has a garage.

5 They did not appoint **either** man as captain.
   Either restaurant would suit me.

6 They appointed **neither** man as captain.
   Neither restaurant is cheap enough.

7 **Such** cheek!
   What fun!
   What a nerve!
   What the heck!

8 He is **such** a nice man!
   What a pleasant surprise this is!
   What the dickens do you mean!

Noun Phrases with several Determiners

Most noun phrases contain only one determiner or none at all, but if there are more, they follow a definite order. Determiners can be divided into four groups, depending on what other determiners they can be used with and the order that they follow.

There are two large groups:
A. *the, this, these, that, those, a(n),* and the possessives *my, your, her, his,* etc. (→ 1).
B. *another, some, any, no, either, neither, each, enough, a few, a little* (→ 2).

These very common words are known as the **central determiners**. A noun phrase will normally contain only one central determiner.

- The group A and group B words cannot be used together, with the exception below.

- Words in group B may be followed by a group A word if *of* is placed between them (→ 3).

- Words in group A can be used in combination with determiners in groups C and D (→ 4).

There are two smaller groups.
C. The smallest group consists of the words: *all, both, half, double,* and *twice.* These can be used on their own before a noun or before the group A determiners above. Some speakers of English prefer to insert *of* between *all, both,* or *half* and a central determiner (→ 5).

- The words in group C are sometimes called **predeterminers**. The exclamatives *such* and *what* belong to this group. See p. 162 for more details about these.

D. The words in the fourth group are, *every, many, several, few, little, much, more, most, less,* the ordinal numbers *first, second, third* etc., and *last.*
These can be used on their own before a noun (→ 6), or after the A group of determiners (→ 7).

1 **a** ripe orange   **my** young sister
   this ripe orange   **our** young sister

2 **each** ripe orange   **another** sister
   some ripe oranges   **enough** money

3 **some** *of* **those** oranges   **neither** *of* **my** sisters

4 **Both** girls were reading.
   Both my young sisters are really sweet.
   All visitors must now leave the ship.
   All the visitors left the ship.

5 **All of the** visitors left the ship.
   Half of the unripe oranges will have to be dumped.

6 **Every** move was carefully recorded.
   She did **many** kind things.
   She has **few** friends.
   First things first, then.
   Last orders, please.

7 **My every** move has been watched.
   The many kind things she did went unreported.
   Her few real friends visited her in hospital.
   His visit was **the first** thing she asked about.
   Those last minutes of the film are horrifying.

Adjectives

Adjectives are used with nouns to make the meaning more specific.

If you use the noun *'bear'* it can mean any animal of that species. As soon as you say *'polar bear'* or *'grizzly bear'* you have given a more specific description; it belongs to this special **class** of bears. If you say *'a large, brown bear'* you have given two of its **attributes**, colour and size, and these qualities might help us select that bear from a lot of others. A noun is said to be **modified** by its adjectives.

Adjectives have two main features:
– Most adjectives can go before a noun; this is termed their **attributive** use (→ 1).
– Most adjectives can go after a link verb such as *be*; this is termed their **predicative** use (→ 2).

Any word that can go into both of these positions is a normal adjective. When used predicatively (after a link verb), an adjective can be either a **subject complement** (→ 2) or an **object complement** (→ 3). See also p. 204.

Adjective Order
The order is normally:
– adjectives that describe feelings or qualities (→ 4).
– adjectives of size, age, temperature, or measurement (→ 5).
– adjectives of colour (→ 6).
– adjectives of nationality or origin (→ 7).
– adjectives denoting substance or material (→ 8).

It is possible to pile up adjectives in English (→ 9), but in practice more than four is most uncommon.

• Adjectives before a noun are not usually separated by *and,* unless they are adjectives of colour (→ 10).

• Adjectives can themselves be premodified by adverbs of degree (→ 11). See also p. 174.

Continued

1 a **tall** girl
   this **green** grass
   four **ill-mannered little** boys
   Both these **fine young thoroughbred** stallions will
   make **a good** price at auction.

2 The grass is **green**.
   The girl grew **tall**.
   These books are **interesting**.

3 Anna painted the room **green**.
   The children drove him **distracted**.

4 **pleasant** childhood memories
   graceful brown hands

5 some **hot** scones   those **hot round** biscuits
   those **nice young** girls   a **nice big** brown biscuit

6 those **pale** girls   some little **brown** biscuits
   her beautiful **blue** eyes

7 those pale **Spanish** girls
   both the small grey **Irish** horses
   an elegant **French** teapot

8 a large **wooden** tub   an elegant **silver** teapot

9 a **happy young blonde German** girl
   beautiful old pink East-Anglian half-timbered
   houses

10 the four **green and white** Chinese paper fans
   a tiny **red and blue** flag

11 an *extremely* **intelligent** student
   a *very* **tall** man
   a *fairly* **untidy** flat

Adjectives (ctd)

Some adjectives can only be used predicatively. Many of the members of this group begin with **a**-: *afloat, afraid, alike, alive, alone, ashamed, asleep, awake* (→ 1).

When an adjective is used predicatively it may have to be followed by a particular preposition if the phrase continues (→ 2). There are some adjectives such as *devoid (of)*, *intent (on)* that must have a following phrase.

Although attributive adjectives usually come before the noun that they modify, there are some that can go immediately after the noun, particularly when they are used with plural nouns, e.g. *absent, present, involved, concerned*. When these adjectives are used in this position they may have a different meaning from the one that they have when they come before the noun (→ 3).

- There are some set phrases which always have an adjective immediately after the noun (→ 4).

Premodifiers and Postmodifiers

Adjectives, determiners, and other nouns can all be used to describe a noun more specifically; that is, they can be used as **modifiers**. Nouns can also be modified by prepositional groups (groups of words that begin with a preposition) and relative clauses added after the noun. See p. 238 for more about relative clauses.

To make it simpler to talk about any modifying word which comes in front of a noun, we can use the term **premodifier** (→ 5). Those modifiers that come after the noun, are called **postmodifiers** (→ 6).

1   Our balloon was **aloft** at last.
    Charles is **abroad** again.
    The child is **afraid**.
    The girls were **asleep** and were not **aware** of the noise.

2   She was glad.   She was **glad to** help.
    He was afraid.   He was **afraid for** his life.
    I was free.   I was **free from** guilt.
    It is **devoid of** interest. He was **intent on** his task.

3   The **girls present** were given tea.
    The **present government** has been in power for a
    long time.
    The **people absent** from work were all ill.
    Let us toast **absent friends**.
    The **dealers concerned** were sent to jail.
    There were letters from **concerned parents**.

4   the **Princess Royal**   a **lion rampant**
    the **president elect**   the **Attorney General**

5   **a young** man   **these** onions
    my aunt's house   **the elephant** house

6   the young man **with the guitar**
    the person **who met me**
    the girl **I was standing near**
    the people **involved**

Comparison

The **comparative** form of an adjective is commonly used
to compare two people, things, or states, when you want to
say that one thing has a larger or smaller amount of a
quality than another.

- If the second part of the comparison is mentioned it
  follows **than** (→ 1).

- Comparison in which you are considering whether two
  people or things are equal is shown by using **as...as** in
  the affirmative and **not as...as** or **not so...as** in the
  negative (→ 2).

The **superlative** form is used for more than two people,
things, or states, when one thing has qualities that exceed
all the others. Superlative adjectives have **the** in front of
them but it can be omitted in predicative positions (→ 3).

There are two ways in which the comparative and
superlative forms of adjectives are formed:

A. You add **-er** or **-est** to the adjective. Adjectives with one
syllable usually add these endings. (→ 4).

- If the word already ends in **-e**, the **-e** must be left off. If a
  word ends in **-y**, it usually adds **-er** or **-est** (**-y** changes to
  -i before adding the ending) (→ 5).

B. You add the word **more** or **most** in front of the adjective.
Adjectives with three syllables or more use **more** or **most**
in front of the adjective (→ 6). So usually do adjectives
formed from participles. To indicate the opposite of both
the **-er / -est** and the **more / most** forms of comparison,
less or **least** is always used (→ 7).

- Adjectives with two syllables (including those that
  already end in **-er**) can follow either pattern or sometimes both patterns. If you are doubtful about a two-
  syllable adjective, use the **more / most** pattern (→ 8).

A small group of irregular adjectives have quite different
spellings for the comparative and superlative forms (→ 9).

1 Anna is **taller than** Mary but Mary is **older**.
   Emma is much **browner than** when I last saw her.
   I've found a card that is **less expensive than** that.

2 Helen is **as tall as** Linda, but **not as sturdy**.

3 That is **the smallest** camera I have ever seen.
   He gave **the least expensive** of the gifts to his sister.
   You can give me whichever apple is (the) **ripest**.

	Comparative	*Superlative*
4 bright	**brighter**	the **brightest**
nice	**nicer**	the **nicest**
sharp	**sharper**	the **sharpest**
5 wise	**wiser**	the **wisest**
pretty	**prettier**	the **prettiest**
weary	**wearier**	the **weariest**
6 fortunate	**more** fortunate	the **most** fortunate
relevant	**more** relevant	the **most** relevant
provoking	**more** provoking	the **most** provoking
enthralled	**more** enthralled	the **most** enthralled
7 sharp	**less** sharp	the **least** sharp
fortunate	**less** fortunate	the **least** fortunate
interesting	**less** interesting	the **least** interesting
involved	**less** involved	the **least** involved
8 shallow	**shallower**	the **shallowest**
or	**more** shallow	the **most** shallow
polite	**politer**	the **politest**
or	**more** polite	the **most** polite
doubtful	**more** doubtful	the **most** doubtful
9 good	**better**	the **best**
bad	**worse**	the **worst**
far	**further**	the **furthest**

Adverbs and Adverbials

When you want to add information about *how, when, where,* or *to what extent* something has happened, you can use an **adverbial**. Many adverbials are members of the group of words called **adverbs,** but adverbials are not necessarily just single words. They can also be word groups, prepositional phrases, or even clauses (→1). They are sometimes called **adjuncts**.

Adverbials generally modify the meaning of a verb (→ 1), an adjective (→ 2), another adverb (→ 3), a whole sentence (→ 4), or a prepositional phrase (→ 5).

Most adverbials are optional parts of a clause or phrase, but there are a few verbs that need an adverb to complete their meaning. See p. 174. Conditional sentences must also have an adverbial clause, usually one beginning with *if* or *unless*. See p. 236 for more about adverbial clauses.

Adverbials can be divided into:
– adverbials of **manner,** which express *how*: e.g. *slowly, with care, well* (→ 6).
– adverbials of **place,** which express *where*: e.g. *there, here, up, in town* (→ 7).
– adverbials of **time,** which express *when*: e.g. *now, today, last night, lately* (→ 8).
– adverbials of **degree,** which express *to what extent*: e.g. *largely, extremely, much, by a whisker* (→ 9).
– adverbials of **frequency,** which express *how often*: e.g. *rarely, often, sometimes, twice daily* (→ 10).

Continued

1 We **greatly** admire your recent paintings.
   The spider scrambled **hurriedly** *into a corner*.
   Monica hummed **softly** *as she ironed her shirt*.
   The firework exploded **with a loud bang**.
   He ran **over the lawn** *towards the nest*.

2 Harry is **particularly** afraid of spiders.
   You must admit that they can be **rather** unnerving.
   That is **quite** silly.
   Fears like that are **very** real to the sufferer.

3 I am **quite** seriously annoyed with you.
   Te government is behaving **remarkably** stupidly.
   Ali objected **very** strongly to the amended wording.

4 **Frankly**, I think he is lying.
   Nevertheless, we must give him a chance.
   Honestly, I didn't mean to be rude to you. **However**, I
   know that it sounded as if I did.

5 The room is **really in an awful mess**.

6 Two men were working their way **slowly** up the hillside.

7 Two men were working their way **up the hillside**.

8 Two men were lost on the hills **yesterday.**

9 It was **largely** their own fault.

10 Search parties went out **every hour**.

Adverbs and Adverbials (ctd)

Although adverbials change the meaning of clauses or phrases, they are usually optional parts of the group or clause (→ 1). They stand outside the word, group, or clause that they are associated with. For example, the same prepositional phrase can in one sentence be part of the description of a noun (a postmodifier), while in another sentence, it may modify the whole clause (→ 2).

The exceptions are that:

– some verbs must be followed by an adverbial to complete their meaning (→ 3).

– some verbs require both an object and an adverbial to complete their meaning (→ 4). See also p. 202.

• New meanings can be made by the combination of an adverbial with a verb to make a phrasal verb (→ 5). See also p. 66 for more about phrasal verbs.

Adverbials are classified according to the way they modify a word, group or clause. In addition to the uses given on p. 172, one important use of a special group of adverbials is to link sentences together by showing that one sentence amplifies, contradicts, or qualifies another. An adverb used in this way is called a **sentence adverb** or a **conjunct** (→ 6).

Another use of adverbials is to let your listener or reader know your point of view about a situation. This is called a **viewpoint adverb** or **disjunct** (→ 7).

A further group of adverbials, all of them adverbs of degree, can only be used with adjectives or other adverbs. Examples are *very, rather, quite, really, too, somewhat*. These are sometimes called **submodifiers** because they can weaken or strengthen the descriptive value of the adjective (→ 8). They are used mainly with adjectives of quality. An adverb can also be submodified by another adverb (→ 9).

Continued

1 He coughed **tentatively**.
   Really, I think you are mistaken.
   In a fit of temper, he slammed the door shut.

2 **A hole *in a nutshell*** means that a grub has got in.
   The problem, **in a nutshell**, is of her own making.

3 Alice behaved **wonderfully**.
   Sylvia acted **unlawfully**.
   Justin sped **down the corridor**.

4 Ranjit put the folder **back**.
   James stood the clubs **in the corner**.
   Clare placed the cover **over the cot**.

5 The car *pulled* out.
   Lydia *went* away.
   Things *are looking* up.

6 **Nevertheless**, we must give him an answer.
   However, it's good advice.
   On the other hand, we cannot turn him down.

7 **Foolishly**, I gave him my address.
   Clearly, he deserves our help.
   Actually, I don't mind.

8 She seems **rather** nice.
   Bert is a **very** good sport.
   Kim gave me this **really** expensive present.

9 The music was being played **quite loudly**.
   Phillipa had been **too easily** impressed.
   It must have been done **extremely recently**.
   The car was **almost totally** submerged in the flood-waters.

Adverbs and Adverbials (ctd)

There are certain adverbs (and adverbials) which can only be used with verbs and so cannot modify adjectives.

A. Most adverbs are able to come:
– before the verb phrase or the subject ($\rightarrow$ 1)
– after the verb phrase or the object ($\rightarrow$ 2)
– between the auxiliary and the main verb ($\rightarrow$ 3).

B. Some adverbs can only come **after** the verb ($\rightarrow$ 4),
e.g. *back, up, down, sideways, clockwise.*

C. A few adverbs can come **before** the main verb ($\rightarrow$ 5),
e.g. *barely, hardly, little, rarely, scarcely, seldom.*
A subordinate clause that begins with one of these words adopts the same word order as a question. These are called **broad negatives,** because they give a negative meaning to a clause ($\rightarrow$ 6).

• Some speakers take care not to place an adverb between the *to* and the **base form** of the verb in a '*to* **infinitive**'. This is called a 'split infinitive'. There is no good reason to regard a split infinitive as an error; the choice is a matter of personal preference ($\rightarrow$ 7).

Adverbs with nouns and pronouns

While **adverbs** can modify most parts of speech, they normally do not modify **nouns** or **pronouns**. Much more common is the use of an adverb of degree to modify a whole **noun phrase** ($\rightarrow$ 8).
There are a few exceptions; a small group of adverbs can modify nouns ($\rightarrow$ 9) or indefinite pronouns ($\rightarrow$ 10).

1 **Happily** she ran over the sand dunes.
   Tearfully, he told his brother the whole story.

2 She ran **happily** over the sand dunes.
   He was telling the whole story **tearfully** to his brother.

3 She was **happily** running about over the sand dunes.
   He was **tearfully** telling the whole story to his brother.

4 Suddenly the frightened animal ran **back**.
   The crab scuttled **sideways / under the rock**.
   They hammered the wedge **in edgeways**.

5 **Scarcely had she spoken** when it came crashing down.
   He **had hardly eaten** a mouthful before the phone rang.
   She **little cared** for his problems.

6 *Compare:*
   They **never noticed** her presence.
   They **scarcely noticed** her presence.

7 to **boldly** go   to go **boldly**
   I need to **really** think hard about this.
   I **really** need to think hard about this.

8 Dominic thought that Geoffrey was **rather a good teacher**.
   Jason is **quite a clever craftsman**.
   She had **scarcely a minute** before the train left.

9 the **man downstairs**   the **example above**
   the value of the **pound abroad**

10 **Almost everyone** brought a bottle to the party.

Form of Adverbs

Most **adverbs** are formed by adding *-ly* to the end of the related adjective (→ 1). Exceptionally, words which end in *-ble* drop off the *-e* before *-ly* is added. So do the words *true* and *due* (→ 2).

- A common spelling mistake is to add *-ley*. This mistake is often made when the adjective ends in the letter *-e*. note the correct spelling of adverbs formed from adjectives ending in *-e* (→ 3).

Adjectives that end in *-y* change to *-i* before adding *-ly*, unless, like *sly* or *wry,* they have only one syllable (→ 4).

Some adverbs keep the same spelling as the adjective to which they are related. It is often difficult to tell at first whether the word is an adjective or an adverb. The general rule is to look at the other words with which it occurs. If it comes before a noun it is probably an adjective (→ 5). If it relates to a verb or an adjective it is probably an adverb (→ 6).

Some adverbs have the same spelling as a preposition. They can be told apart if you look at the words they are found with. Prepositions are normally used in front of noun phrases, because prepositions must have an object (→ 7). When the word is found without an object, especially at the end of a clause, it will usually be an adverb (→ 8).

Just like certain adjectives, some adverbs have comparative and superlative forms and can be used with submodifiers (→ 9). Superlative forms of adverbs are quite rare.

1 slow   slowly
   clever   cleverly
   perennial   perennially

2 sensible   sensibly
   suitable   suitably
   true   truly
   due   duly

3 extreme   extremely
   divine   divinely
   free   freely

4 happy   happily
   greedy   greedily
   sly   slyly

5 a **short way**   a **late meeting**
   a **long pause**   an **early lecture**

6 He **was cut short**.   We **met late**.
   Don't **stay long**.   He **came in early**.

7 He hastened **in a vain attempt** to catch his bus.
   She hurried **over her meal** because she was late.

8 He hastened **in**.
   She hurried **over**.

9 Kim treated Sharon **well**, Karen **less well** and Janice
   the least well.
   Malcolm walked **the most slowly** of all of them.
   Tariq acted **very kindly** towards him.
   You must behave **far more prudently** in future.

Pronouns

A **pronoun** is a word that is used in the place of a noun or a whole noun phrase.

Pronouns are commonly used:
– in place of a noun or a noun phrase that has already been mentioned, when the repetition of the noun or noun phrase would be very strange (→ 1).
– when we know perfectly well who or what is referred to. When, for example, I use the pronoun *I* it is because it would be unusual to refer to myself by name (→ 2).
– when the name of someone or something is not known (→ 3).

Types of pronoun
There are seven different types of pronoun, classified according to their meaning and use.

The **personal** pronouns can be used as subject or object in a clause (→ 4).
The **reflexive** pronouns are used in object position when the action of a verb is performed on the subject by the subject. They are obligatory with certain verbs (→ 5).
Reflexive pronouns are also used for emphasis (→ 6).
The **possessive** pronouns indicate ownership (→ 7).
The **demonstrative** pronouns indicate items that are near to or far from us (→ 8).
The **relative** pronouns are used to link a modifying clause to a noun phrase or to a clause (→ 9).
The **interrogative** pronouns are used to ask a question about the noun phrase they stand in for (→ 10).
The **indefinite** pronouns are used for a broad range of reference when it is not necessary or else not possible to use a personal pronoun (→ 11).

1 Sam has to go to Gatwick. Can you give **him** a lift?
   The newly elected President came out on to the balcony. **He** saluted the crowd.
   The mechanic tested the starter motor. **It** would not work. **He** tried **it** again.

2 **He**'s doing **it** again.
   They have just rung to say that **they** are not coming.

3 **He** was a shabby little man of about fifty in a torn raincoat.
   That has come off the machine again. What is **it** for?

4 **He** gave **her** a box of chocolates.
   They saw **them** both on Friday.
   I can see **you**.

5 The puppy entangled **itself** in the lead.
   I have cut **myself** on this piece of glass.

6 I'll do it **myself**.
   The professor **himself** did not know the answer.

7 Give it back, it's **mine**.
   Perhaps it really is **theirs** after all.

8 **This** is Betty's and **that** is Peter's.
   These are nice. Where did you find them?

9 I don't know **what** you mean.
   That student is the one **who** came top.

10 **What** would you like for lunch?
   Which is the fresh milk?
   Who was responsible?

11 **Everyone** had a compass and a whistle.
   Neither wanted to give way and apologize.
   Much needs to be done.

Personal Pronouns

Personal pronouns are used as the subject, object, or complement in a clause. They are commonly found taking the place of a noun phrase when it is mentioned for a second time.

We use the first-person pronoun *I* to take the role of speaker.
The second-person pronoun *you* is used to allocate the role of listener.
In the case of *you*, there is only one pronoun to cover the singular and the plural, so that it is sometimes necessary to use a form of words that will make clear who is being addressed (→ 1).

When more than one personal pronoun is used with a verb, the order is normally: 3rd or 2nd Person before 1st Person; 2nd Person before 3rd Person (→ 2).

- When two pronouns or a personal noun and a personal pronoun are the joint subject of a verb, the subject form of the pronouns must be used. Avoid the common mistake of saying, for example, *Jerry and me are...* (→ 3).
  When either two pronouns or a noun plus a personal pronoun are the joint object of a verb, the object form of the pronoun must be used (→ 4).

- The object form of a pronoun is used after a preposition. Avoid the common mistake of saying, for example, *between you and I* (→ 5).

The object form is usual in spoken informal usage:
– after the verb *be* (→ 6).
– after *than* (and without *be*) in comparisons (→ 7).

In formal English, the subject form is used where the verb *be* is present or possible (→ 6), (→ 7). Otherwise, *than* + **object** pronoun is necessary (→ 8).

- The object form is also used to supply short answers to questions (→ 9).

Person	*Singular*		*Plural*	
	subject	object	subject	object
1st	I	me	we	us
2nd	you	you	you	you
3rd Masculine	he	him	they	them
3rd Feminine	she	her	they	them
3rd Neutral	it	it	they	them

1 **You** should be ashamed.
All of you should be ashamed.
You must **all** stop writing now.

2 **She and I** do not get along together very well.
You and he should buy the boat between you.

3 **Jerry and I** are going to paint the boat this autumn.
He and **I** are going to paint the boat.
Melanie and **I** are going to town.

4 They decided to help **Jane and me**.

5 Between **you** and **me**, I don't like this place.
Wasn't that kind of **me**?

6 It's **me**.   *Informal*
It is **I**.   *Formal*
I saw at once that it was **her**. *Informal*
I saw at once that it was **she**. *Formal*

7 John is smaller **than him**.   *Informal*
John is smaller **than he (is)**. *Formal*
Sylvia is cleverer **than me**. *Informal*
Sylvia is cleverer **than I (am)**. *Formal*

8 Her results impressed Marcus more **than** (they impressed) **me**.

9 Who found Gran's watch? – **Me**. Aren't I clever!
Did you see who it was? – **Them**, of course.

Reflexive Pronouns

Reflexive pronouns are used:
– when the speaker or writer is referring to an action that
  he or she has caused to happen and of which he or she
  is the object ($\rightarrow$ 1).
– when the direct object or prepositional object of a
  sentence has the same reference as the subject ($\rightarrow$ 2).

The reflexive pronouns are spelled *-self* (singular), *-selves*
(plural).
The reflexive form *oneself* can be used to refer to persons
in general ($\rightarrow$ 3). It can also be used as a substitute for the
1st person singular. If it is used like this, the subject
pronoun should be *one*. In normal direct speech this usage
is often felt to be rather pretentious ($\rightarrow$ 4).

• Avoid mixing *one* or *oneself* in the same clause with *I*
  or *myself*.

Some verbs are always followed by a reflexive pronoun ($\rightarrow$ 5).
Some verbs take an optional reflexive pronoun ($\rightarrow$ 6).
The reflexive pronoun can be left out if it is obvious that
the subject was performing the action of the verb on him-
or herself ($\rightarrow$ 7). The reflexive pronoun is put in if the verb
must have an object i.e. to make the verb transitive ($\rightarrow$ 8).

When a preposition is followed by a pronoun, the pronoun
is normally in the object form ($\rightarrow$ 9). If that pronoun refers
to the subject or object of the main verb, however, it must
be a reflexive pronoun ($\rightarrow$ 10).

• The reflexive can also be used to make some clauses
  more emphatic. To make a strong point, we sometimes
  use a normal subject or object pronoun and a reflexive
  pronoun as well ($\rightarrow$ 11).

The compound pronouns *each other* and *one another* are
not true reflexives. They are used when two or more
subjects mutually take part in an action ($\rightarrow$ 12). They are
sometimes called **reciprocals**.

Person	*Singular*	*Plural*
1st	myself	ourselves
2nd	yourself	yourselves
3rd Masculine	himself	themselves
3rd Feminine	herself	themselves
3rd Neuter	itself	themselves
General	oneself	

1 I cut **myself** badly with the carving knife.
Sometimes I just do not like **myself** very much.

2 John looked at **her**.   John looked at **himself**.
John dressed **himself** in his most formal suit.

3 One ought to keep **oneself** as warm as possible this
winter.

4 One asks **oneself** whether it is worth the bother.
One owes it to **oneself** to do something worthwhile.

5 You should avail **yourself** of the opportunity.

6 Jeremy introduced **himself**. The cat washed **itself**.

7 Jeremy **washed** and **dressed**, then went out.

8 Watch **yourself** in there. It's dangerous.
She was unable to help **herself**.

9 They all looked at **him** as he played the last stroke.

10 She spoke aloud to **herself**. "Just look at **yourself**."
I found myself introducing her to **herself**.

11 Jack, **himself**, placed no trust in doctors.
I will do it **myself**.

12 The apes groomed **one another**.
The lovers embraced **each other**.

Possessive Pronouns

Possessive pronouns are used when you want to indicate who owns or is associated with an item ($\rightarrow$ 1). There are separate forms for the singular and the plural except in the 2nd person. In the 3rd person singular the form changes to match the gender of the possessor ($\rightarrow$ 2).

	Singular	*Plural*
1st	mine	ours
2nd	yours	yours
3rd Masculine	his	theirs
3rd Feminine	hers	theirs
3rd Neuter	its	theirs

- Note that none of these words should be spelled with an apostrophe. Avoid the common mistake of writing *it's* for the possessive form. *It's* is a short form for *it is*.

The Demonstrative Pronouns

The **demonstrative pronouns** are used instead of a noun phrase to indicate position in space (in terms of *near* and *far*) in relation to the speaker, or they can be used to indicate distance in time. They also indicate grammatical number – singular or plural.

	Singular	*Plural*
near	this	these
far	that	those

- Note that the demonstrative pronouns have the same spelling as demonstrative determiners. See also p.154. Usually a demonstrative pronoun substitutes for a noun phrase that contains the same word being used as a determiner ($\rightarrow$ 3).

- It is regarded as impolite to use a demonstrative pronoun to refer directly to a person, except when making introductions ($\rightarrow$ 4) or when beginning a telephone conversation ($\rightarrow$ 5).

1 All those books are **hers**.
   I can tell from the markings that these golf balls are
   ours.
   Have you found any **of mine**?
   Hilda and Esmond, those dreadful cousins **of yours**,
   are here.
   Ours are much nicer.

2 Can you see Helen's tennis shoes? Perhaps these are
   hers.
   Her husband is so dreadful I think that they must
   have bathroom towels labelled **hers** and **its**.
   These are our seats and the ones two rows down are
   theirs.

3 Would you like to share some of this pizza with me?
   Would you like to share **this** with me?
   I would like you to wash those dishes before we go.
   I would like you to wash **those** before we go.

4 John, **this** is Harry Merchant, my colleague.
   This is my secretary, Gordon Smith.
   Mum, **this** is my form teacher, Miss Evans.

5 Good morning, **this** is Speedline Carriers, can we help
   you?
   This is 91 606622. Who do you wish to speak to?

Relative Pronouns

The relative pronouns are the words *who, whom, which,* and *that*. All but *that* have the same form as the interrogative pronouns. See p. 190. The function of a relative pronoun is to link a subordinate clause to a main clause (→ 1). A subordinate clause introduced by a relative pronoun is called a **relative clause**.

Relative pronouns refer back to a noun phrase or pronoun that has just been mentioned. This is called the **antecedent** of the relative pronoun. It is usually the nearest noun phrase or pronoun. All relative pronouns must come as near as possible to the start of the clause that they are in. The only words that normally come before them in the clause are prepositions or conjunctions.

The choice of relative pronoun is influenced as follows:
- *That* as a relative pronoun never has a preposition before it (→ 2).
- *Which* is not used for human subjects or objects (→ 3).
- *Who* and *whom* are restricted to human antecedents (→ 4).
- In **defining** relative clauses (see p. 238), *that* can be used instead of *which* and is sometimes used instead of *who* or *whom*. If the clause is a **non-defining** relative clause, or if there is any possible ambiguity, *who* or *whom* should be used (→ 5).

The **object** form of the relative pronoun is used as the object of a verb or a preposition, but because *whom* is very formal (→ 6), it is not often used: in everyday English, *who* is usually used instead (→ 7).

- In informal writing and speech, any **preposition** is placed after the verb phrase instead of before the relative pronoun (→ 8).

- The object form of a relative pronoun can be left out entirely if the noun referred to is unambiguous (→ 9).

	Personal	*General*
Subject	who *or* that	which *or* that
Object	whom *or* that	which *or* that
Possessive	whose	whose

1 *He might lose his job*, **which** would be a pity.
  She promised *to repay the loan*, **which** I am sure she
  will.

2 That is *a kind thought*, **for which** I am grateful.
  This is *the person* **that** Annie was talking about.
  This is *the person* **about whom** Annie was talking.

3 That is *the car* **which** she has just bought.
  I have found *a ring* **which** you will love.

4 He introduced me to *his friend*, **who** had just
  returned from China.
  I liked *the actress* **who** was playing Masha.

5 I have found *a ring* **which** you will love.
  I have found *a ring* **that** you will love.
  She is *the girl* **who** was at Sam's party.
  She is *the girl* **that** was at Sam's party.

6 The late **Principal** of the College, **whom** we all
  remember with affection, left this bursary in her will.

7 I discovered **who** he was visiting.   *Informal*
  I discovered **whom** he was visiting.   *Formal*

8 The girl **who** Brian was talking **to** seemed agitated.
  The people **who** he had been working **for** that summer
  had offered him a permanent job.

9 He is the *person* Annie was talking about.
  That is the *car* she has just bought.

Interrogative Pronouns

The **interrogative pronouns** *who*, *whom*, and *whose* are used only for reference to people. The interrogative pronouns *which* and *what* can be used for reference to people and things ($\rightarrow$ 1). Interrogative pronouns allow us to build a question around the thing that the pronoun refers to ($\rightarrow$ 1). See p. 210, where they are explained more generally under the heading of **WH-** words.

Who is used to ask questions about people in general ($\rightarrow$ 2).

What is used to ask questions about things in general when the answer is an open one ($\rightarrow$ 3). It is normally only used about people as if you had asked *what occupation* ($\rightarrow$ 4). *What* can be either a subject or an object in a clause ($\rightarrow$ 3).

Which is used to ask for identification of a particular person or a particular thing in a group when you believe that the answer will select something or someone from the group ($\rightarrow$ 5).

Whose is the possessive form of the pronoun. It is used when a person is the possessor ($\rightarrow$ 6). When we want to refer to something as the 'possessor', we use *what* with a suitable verb ($\rightarrow$ 7).

- *Whom* is the object form of *who*. It can be regarded as a very formal word and one which most speakers avoid using in casual conversation, when *who* could be used instead. When writing, however, it is usual to use *whom* ($\rightarrow$ 8).

- The object forms of the interrogative pronoun are also used after a preposition. Informal usage places the preposition at the end of the clause and is the most common ($\rightarrow$ 9).

	Subject	Object	Possessive
General	who	whom	whose
Selective	which	which	
	what	what	

1 **Who** is dancing with Lucy?
   Which is the best book you have read this year?
   What does Mrs Thatcher do when she takes a holiday?
   Whose are these clothes?

2 **Who** is that man over there?
   Who did this?
   Who controls the day-to-day running of the business?

3 **What** opens this door?
   What did you buy for lunch?

4 **What** is her husband? – He's a teacher.

5 **Which** do you want, Indian or China tea?
   Which is the way to open this box?
   Which is your favourite poet, Browning or Coleridge?

6 **Whose** is the Jaguar out there?
   They've judged the roses. **Whose** have won the prize?

7 **What** does this belt **go with**?
   What does this piece **belong to**?

8 **Who** do you have in mind?
   Who were you speaking **to**?
   Formal
   Whom have you in mind?
   To whom were you speaking?

9 **What** do you attribute your success **to**? *Informal*
   To what do you attribute your success? *Formal*

Indefinite Pronouns

The indefinite pronouns are used in a general sense when you do not know or do not need to say precisely who or what you are referring to. The noun phrase for which they substitute can refer to a person, a thing, or a group of persons or things, in which gender and number are not made clear (→ 1).

The indefinite pronouns can be grouped according to meaning, as follows:

A. General amounts and quantities: *most, some, none, any, all, both, half, several, enough, many, each* (→ 2).

B. Choice or alternatives: *either, neither* (→ 3).

C. Undefined singular or multiple persons and things:

someone	*somebody*	*something*
no one	*nobody*	*nothing*
anyone	*anybody*	*anything*
everyone	*everybody*	*everything*

- Note the form of *no one* or, less usually, *no-one*.

- The pronouns in group C that refer to people can cause problems concerning the **number** and **gender** of a following determiner or pronoun. Formal usage permits only the use of a following **singular** form. Common practice, which is increasingly accepted, uses the plural form *their* or *theirs* and avoids awkward expressions like *his or her* (→ 4).

Many of these pronouns, especially those in groups A and B, have the same form as determiners. See p. 146.

- The way to tell them apart is to see if the word on its own is used as a subject, an object, or the complement of a verb; this is a **pronoun**. If, on the other hand, it is used in front of a noun, it is a **determiner** (→ 5).

- The pronouns in Groups A and B are often used like partitives, with *of* and a noun phrase or a personal pronoun (→ 6).

1 **Someone** will have to tell Harriet that she has failed.
   Everybody had a wonderful time.
   Anything is better than nothing.
   Nothing can make up for this loss.
   Others may say unkind things, but I never will.
   Several of them were going on to another party.

2 **Many** find his books objectionable.
   All in the Party respect his motives.
   Judging by the comments, **most** wanted her to stay on.
   We have lost a lot of our property in a fire, **some** was
   saved.
   Enough has been said on this topic to fill a book.

3 Please bring me one of those spanners. **Either** will do.
   Neither was ready for the truth when it came.

4 Has **anybody** finished **his or her** lunch yet?
   Everybody applauded **his or her** own son.
   Everybody applauded **their** own son.
   Has **anybody** finished **their** lunch yet?
   Has **anyone** finished **theirs** yet?

5 *As a pronoun:*
   Both were awarded a valuable prize.
   Several got through the fence.
   I have found **some**.
   As a determiner:
   Both men were saved from the wreckage.
   Several sheep got through the fence.
   I have found **some scrap paper**.

6 **None** of the children were hurt, but **most** of them
   were rather upset.
   Neither of his parents loved him.

Prepositions

A preposition is one of a small but very common group of
words that relate different items to each other. Most
English prepositions have a number of meanings that are
particular to each preposition.

Simple prepositions consist of one word, e.g. *in, on, under.*
Complex prepositions consist of more than one word,
e.g. *due to, together with, on top of, in spite of, out of.*

Prepositions enable us:
– to express movement to or from a **place.**
– to express **location** and **time**.

Prepositions are normally followed by:
– a noun phrase (→ 1).
– an *-ing* clause (→ 2).
– a relative pronoun (**WH-** word). In informal speech a
  preposition may end a relative clause rather than come
  before it (→ 3). See also p. 238.

A preposition needs an object, rather like a transitive verb.
A preposition and the noun phrase that goes with it is
called a **prepositional phrase**. A prepositional phrase is
used as an **adverbial** (→ 4) or a **postmodifier** (→ 5).

• Prepositions combine with some verbs to make new
  meanings from the combination. These are one type of
  phrasal verb (→ 6). See p. 66.

The list on the facing page is of all the common simple
prepositions (→ 7). Some words are either **prepositions** or
adverbs, depending on how they are used and what they
combine with. The words in *italics* can also be used as
adverbs. Example 8 shows adverbial uses (→ 8).

Continued

1 in **time**   over **the edge**
   under **the table**   together with **my friends**

2 Thanks **for looking**.
   It is good if you can have pride **in working for us**.

3 That's the person **of whom** we were speaking.
   I saw the man **to whom** I gave the packet yesterday.
   The person (**who**) we were speaking **of**.
   That's the man (**who**) I gave the packet **to**.

4 He put the flowers **on the table**.
   She shut the dog **in the kitchen**.
   He found the papers **in time for the meeting**.

5 **The house** *on the corner* **has at last been sold.**
   The flowers *on the table* **are from Tim.**
   A bird *with brilliant plumage* **roamed the lawns.**

6 I **believe in** his innocence.   I **stand for** justice.
   She **went through** a bad patch.

7 *aboard, about, above, across, after*, against, *along,
   alongside*, amid, among, *around*, as, at, atop, bar,
   before, behind, below, beneath, beside, between, beyond,
   by, despite, *down* during, for, from, *in, inside*, into, like,
   near, of, *off, on*, onto, *opposite, outside, over, past*,
   pending, per, prior, pro, re, regarding, *round*, since,
   than, *through, throughout*, till, to, towards, *under,
   underneath*, until, unto, *up*, upon, via, with, *within,
   without*.

8 He went **in**.   I took it **through**.

Prepositions (ctd)

When a verb is followed by a preposition there is often little or no choice as to which one to use, e.g. *rely on, speak to, give to*.
When there is a choice of preposition the meaning changes:
check for, check on, check over; speak to, speak about; talk to, talk with.

Prepositions allow us to express relationships. These are mostly to do with place and time. Some prepositions can be used with more than one meaning, depending on how we think about the time or place we are discussing.

Prepositions of location

Prepositions can indicate:
- the direction in which something is moving in relation to another person or thing: *towards, from, off* ($\rightarrow$ 1).
- something or someone being enclosed: *within, in, inside, outside* ($\rightarrow$ 2).
- being at a certain point: *on, at, by, near* ($\rightarrow$ 3).
- place as an area: *over, across, on, onto* ($\rightarrow$ 4).
- location as a line: *along, over, on* ($\rightarrow$ 5).

Prepositions of time

Prepositions can also indicate:
- a point in time or a date : *at, on, in* ($\rightarrow$ 6).
- a period or point of time which marks a change: *before, after, since, until* ($\rightarrow$ 7).
- the duration of some event: *for* ($\rightarrow$ 8).

1 They ran **towards** the station.
   He took the road **from** the town **to** the nearest village.

2 **Within** this box are secrets nobody will ever see.
   There seems to be something loose **inside** the control
   box.
   For this game you have to stand **outside** the room
   while we make up some questions.
   Did you put the cheese back **in** the fridge?

3 Hit the nail right **on** the top.
   I'll meet you **at** the park.
   There is a sawmill **near** where I live.

4 Sid jumped **onto** the back of the lorry.
   He slid the packet **across** the table.
   The air currents flow **over** the Atlantic and affect our
   weather.

5 He looked **along** the line of the fence.
   The rabbit scuttled **over** the road.
   Please sign **on** the dotted line.

6 The baby arrived **at** 9 pm. **on** April 1st.
   It was **in** June that they got married.
   I'll come **in** five minutes.

7 We lived there **before** Mother died.
   I was at that school **until** I turned sixteen.
   I usually go there **after** work.

8 Helen worked there **for** the whole of July.

Word Order in Sentences

The order of words in an English sentence is very important. Word order is a carrier of meaning; a change in word order usually results in a change of meaning.

Many other languages use **inflection,** a change in the form of words, to show how the parts of a sentence fit together. English has very few inflections, so the place that a word occupies in a sentence, its **syntax,** is the most important feature.

Neutral word order

Most sentences have a subject, and then something that is said about the subject, which is usually the rest of the sentence. This divides the sentence into the **subject** and the **predicate** ($\to$ 1). Most sentences put the information that they carry in this order. This is neutral word order. When this neutral order is changed, the meaning of a sentence also changes ($\to$ 2).

Word order in simple sentences

Simple sentences are those which have only one clause. They are extremely common in all forms of written and spoken English. Simple sentences have a normal word order which varies according to whether the sentence is:

- a **statement** ($\to$ 3),
- a **question** ($\to$ 4),
- a **command** ($\to$ 5).

Word order also varies according to whether the sentence is **negative** or **positive**.

Focusing

When we want to focus the attention of a reader or a listener on a particular word or phrase, we can use variations on neutral order, such as putting the subject last, splitting the clause into two, or repeating some part of the sentence ($\to$ 6).

1 John (*subject*) bought the tickets on Saturday
   (*predicate*).
   The wall (*subject*) was torn down (*predicate*).
   My elderly mother (*subject*) is rather deaf (*predicate*).

2 The **cat** killed the dog = the dog died.
   The **dog** killed the cat = the cat died.
   The **child** watched the rabbit.
   The **rabbit** watched the child.

3 **I saw you** at the theatre on Saturday night.
   I didn't see you at the theatre on Saturday night.

4 **Did I see you** at the theatre on Saturday night?
   Didn't I see you at the theatre on Saturday night?

5 You **should buy** a ticket now.
   Shouldn't you buy a ticket now?
   Buy a ticket now.
   Don't buy a ticket now.

6 *Some variations on the theme of neutral word order.*
   The one who bought the tickets was John.
   All John did was to buy the tickets.
   John bought the tickets, didn't he?
   The tickets were bought by John, I think.
   It was on Saturday that John bought the tickets.

Mood

Word order in sentences is connected to **mood**. Each
sentence in English provides some type of information.
For example, a sentence can be a statement, question,
request, command, denial or a response etc. In English
the choice and order of the parts of a sentence, called
mood, help us express these meanings.

Almost all statements and denials are in the **declarative**
mood. An important feature of declarative mood is that
these sentences have a subject that comes before the verb
(→ 1).

Most questions are in the **interrogative** mood. An
important feature of interrogative mood is that these
sentences normally have a subject that comes after an
auxiliary verb (→ 2). If the subject does come first it will
be a special question word (→ 3).

- Exceptionally, we can ask questions using the
  declarative mood. We do this by using a special tone of
  voice (→ 4).

Many commands are in the **imperative** mood. Commands
in the imperative mood have no word that acts as a
subject, though the subject is understood to be *you*.
Commands in the imperative mood can sound rude or
impatient (→ 5).

- We can make a **request,** which is a type of command,
  sound more polite by using the interrogative mood (→ 6).
- Not all imperative mood sentences are orders or
  commands. They can be social expressions (→ 7).

There is also a **subjunctive** mood. This is rarely used in
English now. It may be used when you want to talk about
an improbable or unlikely situation (→ 8).

1 Our dog **eats** any old thing.
   Our dog **won't** just **eat** any old thing.
   The dog **has** already **been fed**.
   The dog **hasn't been fed** yet.
   We **have won** several races in our new yacht.
   We **haven't won** any races in our new yacht.

2 **Does** your dog **eat** any old thing?
   Has the dog already **been fed**?
   Has the dog not **been fed** yet?
   Have you **won** any races in your new yacht?
   Haven't you **won** any races in your new yacht yet?

3 **Who won** the race?
   Which yacht **was** it?

4 **You're telling me** he has a new car? I don't believe it.
   It's raining again? That makes three days running.

5 **Eat** it up!
   Feed the dog, please.
   On your marks, **get set**, ... **go**!

6 **Would you** feed the dog, please.
   Would you mind shutting the door.
   Could I have that now, thank you.

7 **Have** a nice day.
   Get well soon.

8 If I **were** Prime Minister, I'd abolish road tax.

Declarative Mood

The **declarative** mood is used to make statements.
A statement is usually the expression of a fact or of an opinion, as in all the examples. Statements can be both positive or negative. A denial, for example, is a form of negative statement (→ 10). (See also p. 206).

Declarative mood always contains a subject and a following verb phrase. What follows the verb phrase, however, is often controlled by the actual verb that is chosen.

The normal word order in the declarative mood is:

subject + verb phrase (→ 1)
subject + verb phrase + direct object (→ 2)
subject + verb phrase + adverbial (→ 3)
subject + verb phrase + direct object + adverbial (→ 4)

Certain verbs must have following objects, e.g. *see, find, prefer, take* (→ 5). Other verbs need, or can have, both a **direct** and an **indirect** object, e.g. *give, buy, offer* (→ 6). The word order can be either:

subject + verb + indirect object + direct object (→ 5)

or, with the addition of a word that indicates the recipient:

subject + verb + direct object + *to / for* **+ indirect object** (→ 7).

Another group of verbs must be followed either by an object and an adverbial expression, or an adverbial expression on its own e.g. *put, place, stand* (→ 8).

A further type of declarative mood statement (→ 9) has the same basic order of subject and verb as example 2, but with a **complement** replacing the direct object. See p. 204 for more about complements and p. 12 for more objects.

1 Kate is working.
   Tim was reading.
   Helen stared at me in surprise.

2 Ronald is writing a letter.
   Pandora reserved several library books.
   Stephen prefers a vegetarian diet.

3 Dominic was eating very slowly.
   Lyndsey was studying in the library.
   Indira laughed happily.

4 Dominic was eating his lunch very slowly.
   Lyndsey had been reading a magazine in the library.
   Philippa prodded him with her elbow.

5 She saw **her friend**.   He found **a camera.**
   They took **a holiday brochure.**

6 Kate gave *the dog* **a bone**.
   Stuart bought *Maire* **a birthday present**.

7 Kate gave **a bone** *to the dog*.
   Stuart bought **a birthday present** *for Maire*.

8 Richard placed **the computer** *on the table*.
   Diana put **her jeans** *in the drawer*.
   Michael stood *in the middle of the pitch*.

9 Elisabeth seems to have been **very happy** lately.
   This dessert is **delicious**.

10 Kate is not working after all.
   Tim wasn't reading.
   Helen was not staring at you.
   I am not writing a letter.

Complements

Some verbs e.g. *be, become, seem*, do not have an object but a **complement**.

The **subject complement** is a word or phrase that tells us more about the subject (→ 1). The subject complement is linked to the subject by a verb, and the order is as follows:

subject + verb + subject complement

Subject complements may be either noun phrases, pronouns, adjectives, or even prepositional phrases.

- Most adjectives can be used after a group of verbs that includes: *appear, be, become, look, seem, smell, taste*, etc. An adjective that is used in this position is called a **predicative** adjective and it is functioning as a **complement** (→ 2).

Less frequently we find an **object complement**. The object complement tells us more about the direct object. It relates directly to the object and is placed after it (→ 3). Verbs that can take an object complement with their direct object include *make, call*, and *appoint*. The order is as follows:

subject + verb + direct object + object complement

1 Alan is **a nice person**.
   Rajiv is **a male psychiatric nurse**.
   Alison seems **very well balanced**.
   Rosamund is **herself** again.
   The person who broke the window is **him**.
   That's **it**.
   This is for **you**.

2 The tickets seemed **expensive**, but the show was
   excellent.
   These little cakes are **delicious**.
   Soon afterwards, Patrick became **ill**.
   That girl appears **too young to do that job**.

3 That accident made **him** *a poorer man*.
   Peter's phone call made **Maureen** *happy*.
   She called **me** *a fool*.
   They appointed **him** *Director*.

Word Order in Negative Statements

Negative statements usually contain the word *not*. In such sentences, the basic word order for subject and object is the same as in positive statements (→ 1). The difference is that, as well as containing *not*, negative statements must have as part of the verb phrase, either:

– a **primary auxiliary** verb (→ 2),
– one or other of the **modal auxiliary** verbs (→ 3), or
– a form of *be* used as a main verb (→ 4).

The word *not* is added right after the first one of these auxiliary verbs. The main verb follows.

The word order is, therefore:

>   **subject + auxiliary + *not* + main verb.**

A negative sentence may contain a modal verb and one or more primary auxiliaries as well (→ 5). In this case the word order is:

>   **subject + modal + *not* + primary auxiliary + main verb.**

If the verb phrase does not already contain one of these verbs, then it is necessary to add the **supporting auxiliary** verb *do*.

The Simple Present and the Simple Past tenses of main verbs insert the appropriate form of *do* and then add *not* followed by the base form of the main verb (→ 6). See p. 40 for more on the supporting auxiliary. The word order is, therefore:

>   **subject + do- auxiliary + *not* + main verb**

- The contracted form of *not*, which is *n't*, can be used after every auxiliary verb except *am*. This is the most common spoken form (→ 7). The full form with *not* tends to be used more in writing.

- *can + not* is usually written *cannot* (→ 8).

- Other words with a negative meaning, *never, barely, hardly, scarcely, rarely,* do not change the order of words in a statement (→ 9).

1 John has gone to school.
   John has **not** gone to school.

2 She **had not** arrived in time.
   Kate **is not** working.
   Tim **was not** reading.

3 I warn you, he **may not** want to.
   Elsa **could not** see the direction of the road any
   longer.

4 That **is not** my book.

5 I *may not have* gone by then.
   They *could not have* seen her.
   They *should not have been playing* in the road.

6 He runs.   He **does not** run.
   He ran.   He **did not** run.
   Lynn **does not** work overtime now.
   The bus service **did not** run on Sundays.

7 He **doesn't** run.   He **didn't** run.
   Lynn **doesn't** work on Sundays.
   She **hasn't** been to work all week.
   He **isn't** going to come after all.
   Bill went swimming but Ann **didn't** go.

8 She **can't** come.   She **cannot** come.

9 She **doesn't buy** *Vogue*.
   She **never buys** *Vogue*.
   He **barely** earns enough to live on.
   I **hardly** think that is going to be enough.
   I **scarcely** saw my brother last month.

Interrogative Mood

The interrogative mood is normal for many questions.
It contains a verb phrase that is followed by a subject.
There are two main types of question: those that can be
answered *yes* or *no*, and those that have to be answered
with a specific piece of information or a sentence such as
I don't know. Each type of question has its own special
word order.

Polar questions

Questions that expect the answer *yes* or *no* are called
polar questions or sometimes, *yes/no* questions.
The interrogative mood is used to form polar questions.

The normal sentence order for the interrogative mood is:
    modal / auxiliary verb + subject + base form of the
    main verb ($\rightarrow$ 1).

When a sentence does not contain a modal verb or an
auxiliary verb, i.e. a sentence with the main verb in the
Simple Present or Simple Past tense, the question is
formed by placing a form of the supporting auxiliary verb
do before the subject and following it with the **base form**
of the main verb ($\rightarrow$ 2).

Polar questions also have a negative form. **Negative
polar questions** are almost always contracted. The
negative in its contracted form *n't* comes immediately
before the subject ($\rightarrow$ 3). If the full negative form *not* is
used, it comes immediately after the subject. The full form
is very formal ($\rightarrow$ 4).

Non-polar questions

When you want to get a detailed answer, not just *yes* or *no*,
you must use a **non-polar question,** which allows for
many possible answers ($\rightarrow$ 5).
The words *who, whom, whose, what, which, when,
where, why*, and *how* are used to form this sort of
question. These words are referred to as **WH-** words.
See pp. 210–213.

1   **Were** the dogs barking?
    Have the girls been dieting?
    May Ahmed come too?
    Must she go already?
    Would you like a chocolate?

2   **Does** he enjoy tennis?
    Did he play a lot?
    Did that surprise his family?

3   **Doesn't** he like to talk about his old boss?
    Can't Peter have one too?
    Don't you speak French?
    Mayn't a man have a biscuit in his own house?

4   **Does** he **not** like to talk about his former employer?
    Can one **not** live in peace without interruptions all
    day?
    May a man **not** have a biscuit in his own house?

5   *Polar:*
    Did you ring the school? – Yes, I did.
    Was the car serviced yesterday? – No / I don't know.
    Have you seen Ali yet? – Yes, I have.

    Non-polar:
    Who(m) did you ring? – I was ringing the school.
    What happened about getting the car serviced? – It's
    done.
    When did you see Ali? – Last Wednesday.
    Where is Peter going? – To work.
    When did they arrive? – Yesterday.
    Why have you stopped smoking? – I was told to.

WH- Words

The **WH-** words are also called **interrogatives**. They are used for non-polar questions. They can be determiners, adverbs, or pronouns.

WH- determiners

When used as determiners, *what*, *which*, or *whose* can be used to ask questions:
- about nouns (→ 1) or
- about the pronoun *one* or *ones* (→ 2).

- The determiner *which* can be used to select. It can also be used together with the preposition *of* for the same purpose (→ 3).

- The determiner *whose* asks about possession with reference to a person as the possessor (→ 4).

WH- adverbs

The adverb **WH-** words, *when, where, how,* and *why,* always make the sentence follow the interrogative mood word order.

- *When* asks about time (→ 5).
- *Where* asks about place (→ 6).
- *How* asks about manner (→ 7).
- *Why* asks about reasons and purpose (→ 8). Questions with *why* are usually answered with a clause containing *because* to express reason, or with the *to* infinitive to express purpose.
- *How much* implies reference to a quantity; *how many* implies reference to an amount or a countable number of things but may leave out the noun referred to (→ 9).
- *How* can also be used with adjectives such as *old, big, far,* or with adverbs such as *often, soon, quickly* to ask about degree, rate, or timing (→ 10).

Continued

1 **What book** is Maddie reading?
  Which plane is he catching?
  Whose jersey is this?

2 **Which one** would you like?
  Which ones did Ruth want?

3 **Which colour** shall we use?
  Which book sells the most copies?
  Which of these colours shall we use?
  Which of them did the best work?

4 **Whose** mother did you say she was?
  Whose jersey is this?

5 **When** will they arrive?   **When** shall I see you again?

6 **Where** are you going?   **Where** have you been?
  Where is Adlestrop?

7 **How** did you get here? – We came by train.
  How does a computer work?

8 **Why** is the baby crying? – **Because** she is hungry.
  Why are you saving your money? – **To buy** a bicycle.

9 **How much** did they take? – All of it. / The lot.
  How much does it cost? – £4.20.
  How many do you want? – I want twelve of them.
  How many do you want? – Twelve.

10 **How far** is it to the station? – About five kilometres.
   How often does he come? – Not very often.

WH- Words (ctd)

WH- pronouns

The **pronouns** *who, whose, which,* and *what* can be the subject or object of a verb ($\rightarrow$ 1). The interrogative pronoun *whose* is used when the question is asked about a person as the possessor of something ($\rightarrow$ 2). See also pp. 188–190 on interrogative and relative pronouns.

- The form *whom* is used as the object of a verb or of a preposition in very formal written and spoken English ($\rightarrow$ 3). Modern English usage prefers *who* instead of *whom* in all but the most formal contexts ($\rightarrow$ 4).

When *whom* is used as the object of a preposition, it normally follows the preposition ($\rightarrow$ 5). When *who* is used, the preposition is placed at the end of the clause ($\rightarrow$ 6).

The subject **WH-** pronouns are found in the same sentence order as statements:
 WH- subject pronoun + the main verb ($\rightarrow$ 7).

The object **WH-** pronouns make the sentence take the order of interrogative mood, just like polar questions:
 WH- object pronoun + primary or modal auxiliary + subject + base form of the verb ($\rightarrow$ 8).

- There are a few exceptions to this in informal spoken English, used mainly for emphasis ($\rightarrow$ 9).

1 **Who** can help me?
   I don't know **who**.
   Whose is the new raincoat that I saw out there?
   I've no idea **whose** it is.
   Which was your best subject at school?
   I can't say **which**.
   What fell down just then?
   What will Mary take with her to camp?

2 **Whose** was the vintage car I saw at the wedding.
   Whose is this?

3 *Formal and old-fashioned*
   You saw **whom** at the theatre?
   Whom did you see?
   Whom should he send on this mission?

4 You saw **who** at the theatre?
   (**Who** did you see at the theatre?)
   Who should he send on this mission?

5 **To whom** did you give it?
   With whom did you go?

6 **Who** did you give it **to** ?
   Who did you go **with** ?

7 **Who can help** me?
   Whose is the new raincoat that I saw out there?
   Which was your best subject at school?
   What fell down just then?

8 *What will Mary take* with her to camp?
   What has Jonathan caught in the net?

9 You did **what**?

Sentence Tags

Tags are short additions that look like questions, used at the end of a declarative sentence. They are sometimes called **question tags,** but many sentences ending with a tag are not real questions. They are usually used to check that the listener agrees with what the speaker has said. Sentence tags are very commonly used in spoken English, but not in formal written English.

The tag is added to the end of a statement. If the auxiliary verb *be* or *have* or a **modal** verb is part of the verb phrase in the sentence, then it is used as the verb in the sentence tag ($\to$ 1). If the main verb is in the Simple Present or Simple Past tense, the tag is made using *do* ($\to$ 2).

In negative tags, *n't* is added to the auxiliary. Note that this contracted form is always used, even in writing ($\to$ 2), ($\to$ 4), ($\to$ 6).

- The formal forms such as, *does he not, did I not, have you not,* sound old-fashioned. They are less uncommon in some regional varieties of English.

The pronoun in the sentence tag must match the subject of the main verb ($\to$ 3).

Sentence tags can be **negative** ($\to$ 4) or **positive** ($\to$ 5). Normally, when the first part of the sentence is positive, the tag verb will be negative, and vice versa. Sentences in which both verbs have the same polarity, either both parts negative or both positive, are less common. These sentences must be used carefully as, with certain tones of voice, they can sound very aggressive ($\to$ 6).

- The same sentence tag may have different meanings depending on the tone of voice that is used with it ($\to$ 7). In the example the sentence can be a statement of fact or a question, depending on whether your voice rises or falls at the end.

Continued

1 It **isn't** raining again, **is it**?
You**'ve seen** the programme, **haven't you**.
Well, we **can't jump** over it, **can we**.
You **will come**, **won't you**?

2 He certainly **likes** eating, **doesn't he**.
I **slipped up** there, **didn't I**.

3 **You** aren't listening, are **you**? – Of course I am!
Hugh reads a lot, doesn't **he**.

4 They **went** with you, **didn't they**? – No, they didn't.

5 Your father **doesn't belong to** the golf club, **does he**?
– Of course, he does. He's been a member for years.

6 You **think** I'm a fool, **do** you?
You **haven't** used my bicycle, **haven't** you? What's this
big scratch then?

7 *Falling tone: statement*
She's gone out, hasn't she.

Rising tone: question
She's gone out, hasn't she?

Sentence Tags (ctd)

Sentence tags are used in the following combinations:

A. To say something that the speaker expects the listener will agree with. This is usually not a question:

    positive main verb + negative tag (→ 1)

or **negative main verb + positive tag** (→ 2)

B. To point out or remark on something surprising, often something that the listener cannot deny. This frequently sounds more like a question:

    positive main verb + negative tag (→ 3)

or **negative main verb + positive tag** (→ 4)

C. To show interest in something. This often repeats part of what the previous speaker has said:

    positive main verb + positive tag (→ 5)

or **negative main verb + negative tag** (→ 6)

When a tag is used in way C, the sentence is often begun with *So.* This type of tag, especially in the negative form, can also be used in a threatening manner, challenging the listener to agree or disagree (→ 6).

- After a command, a tag made with *can, could, will, shall,* or *would* makes an order more polite (→ 7).

- The punctuation of sentences that end with a tag poses a problem. The main part of the sentence is usually a statement, which should end with a full stop. The tag then asks, 'Is this right?' The tone of voice should be the guide. If the sentence sounds more like a statement, a full stop can be used as punctuation, instead of a question mark.

1   Mary **will pass** her driving test this time, **won't she**.
    Graham **seems** to have lost interest in sailing, **doesn't
    he**.

2   Jessica **didn't care**, **did she**.
    Kerry **hadn't done** sufficient preparation, **had she**.

3   You've just **bought** a new car, **haven't you**?
    Henry **has been** away already this year, **hasn't he**?

4   Desmond **hasn't been** to see you, **has he**?
    Paula **wasn't** in your class at school, **was she** ?

5   You **saw** him in town, **did you**?
    So, you **come** from New Zealand, **do you**?
    So you've just **come back** from skiing, **have you**?

6   Oh, so you've **never seen** her before, **haven't you**?
    You **don't like** my cooking, **don't you**? Well, you do
    some then!

7   Make me a cup of tea, **will you**?
    Just wait a minute, **would you**?
    Let's go to the cinema, **shall we**?

Imperative Mood

Commands and orders

The **imperative** mood is used to give commands and
orders. The form of the verb used for the imperative is the
base form of the main verb, which is used without a
subject (→ 1).

- Although the main feature of sentences in the
  imperative mood is that they have no **grammatical**
  subject, they do have an **understood** subject, '*you*'.

The basic form of the imperative mood remains the same
whether it is addressed to one or more people (→ 2).
There is also a special type of imperative, using *let's*,
that is used when you need to include the speaker.
See p. 220.

The word order of a sentence in the imperative mood is:

verb + object (if needed).

The negative imperative is made with *do + not* or *don't* (→ 3).

The uses of the imperative mood are as follows:
- to give an order (→ 4)
- to give instructions (→ 5)
- to give advice or warnings (→ 6)
- to make an offer or an invitation (→ 7)

The imperative mood of *do* + a **main verb** can be used:
- for emphasis (→ 8)
- to be persuasive (→ 9)
- to show irritation (→ 10)

- Note that the imperative mood is not the only way to
  form a command or an order. You can also issue a
  command when you use a sentence in the declarative
  mood or the interrogative mood (→ 11).

Continued

1 **Walk** to the corner, **turn** right, and **cross** the road.
   Open your mouth and **say** 'Aaaah'.

2 Come on, **Mary.** I'm waiting.
   Come on, **children.** You're late.

3 **Don't lose** that key.
   Do not come back without it, do you understand!

4 **Go** away.
   Stop that.
   Keep quiet.

5 **Do not use** this spray near a naked flame.
   Apply the glue thinly and **leave** it for ten minutes.

6 **Don't forget** to take your passport with you.
   Be careful!
   Don't slip on the icy patch.

7 **Have** a piece of cake.
   Come up and **see** me some time!

8 It is an excellent exhibition; **do go** and see it.

9 **Do try** to eat a little of this; it will be good for you.

10 **Do stop** talking! I'm trying to work.

11 I'm certainly not going to get it – **you get it**
    Would you get it, then? I'm waiting.

Imperative Mood (ctd)

Making suggestions

Let's (*let* + *us*) + **main verb** is used in the first person plural only, especially when you are trying to encourage or entice someone to do something with you.

It includes both the speaker and the hearer, so the subject that is understood is represented by the plural *we* (→ 1).

- Suggestions which start with *let's* often end with the sentence tag *shall we*? (→ 2).

In ordinary English the negative is *let's not* + **main verb** or sometimes *don't let's* + **main verb** (→ 3).
In formal English, the negative is *let us not* + **main verb** (→ 4).

Do let's is the emphatic form (→ 5).

- The uncontracted form *let us* + **main verb** is occasionally used in formal and written English (→ 6).

The answer to a suggestion with *let's* is normally either, *yes, let's* or *no, let's not* or sometimes, *no, don't let's* (→ 7).

1   **Let's visit** Malcolm this weekend.
     Please let's go to the cinema tonight.
     Do let's have a look at your new computer, Chris.
     Let's pool our resources.

2   **Let's phone** her now, **shall we?**
     Let us go for a walk after supper, **shall we?**

3   **Let's not do** the washing up just now.
     Don't let's do the washing up just now.

4   **Let us not alarm** people.

5   It's a very good bargain; **do let's buy** it at once!

6   **Let us get to work** at once.
     Pray **let us** continue.

7   **Let's phone** her now, shall we? – Yes, **let's.**
     Let's phone her now, shall we? – No, **let's not.**
     Let's visit Malcolm this weekend. – No, **don't let's** do that.

The Vocative

The imperative mood is often used with a **vocative**.
This is where you mention a person's name or some other
way of identifying the person to whom a command or
request is being addressed ($\rightarrow$ 1).
The vocative can be a proper noun, the pronoun *you*, or a
noun phrase. The vocative can come before or after the
main clause.

A vocative forms a part of many questions ($\rightarrow$ 2).

A vocative is also combined with an interrogative mood
clause to form a request ($\rightarrow$ 3). Requests are normally used
when the person being addressed has the choice to do or
not do what you are aking.

When a vocative is used with an imperative mood clause,
the sentence is usually a command ($\rightarrow$ 4). A command can
also be phrased as a request ($\rightarrow$ 5).

A practical reason for using a vocative is to supply the
missing but understood subject, so that the right person
will understand the command or request and act on it.

- Note the punctuation. There should be a comma
  between the vocative part of the clause and the
  remainder.

- As part of a command, except for urgent warnings,
  the use of the vocative is considered rude or abrupt.
  A more polite form is *Would you...?* using the
  interrogative mood ($\rightarrow$ 5). When the vocative is a
  pronoun, it has to be *you*. Using *you* as a vocative in a
  command sounds rude and angry ($\rightarrow$ 4).

1 **David**, come here!
   Come here, **David**.
   Would you come here, David.
   That girl in the red coat, stop talking!

2 **Peter**, do you know where I put the video tape?
   Have you seen Clive recently, **Jenny**?

3 **Tony**, would you pass me the hammer?
   Could I speak to you privately for a minute, **Sue**?

4 **Sam**, get off there!
   You, get off there!
   Get off there, **you**!

5 **Would you stop** talking now, darling, and go to sleep.
   Would you get off there, please, Sam.

Subjunctive Mood

The **subjunctive** mood was formerly used in English for situations that were improbable or that expressed a wish. It is only rarely used in modern British English. It is, however, found in certain set phrases (→ 1) and in very formal forms of speech and writing.

The Present Subjunctive

The form in the present tense is exactly the same as the base form in all persons of the verb. That is, there is no *-s* on the 3rd person singular.

The subjunctive is used, in very formal English, in subordinate clauses that follow verbs expressing a desire, a demand, a recommendation, or a resolve (→ 2). The clause containing the subjunctive is linked to the main clause with *that*.

• This use of the subjunctive is more common in American English than in British English. British speakers usually take advantage of other ways of expressing the same message, especially in less formal speech (→ 3).

The Past Subjunctive

In written English and in very formal speech, the past subjunctive form *were* is sometimes used with the first and third person singular, in place of the normal past form *was* (→ 4). The past subjunctive may be used :
– after *if*, to express regret or longing (→ 4)
– after *as if / as though* and similar expressions, to express doubt or improbability (→ 5).

• Many people prefer to use the normal form of the past in this type of sentence. This is quite acceptable in ordinary English (→ 6).

1 God **save** the Queen!   God **bless** you!
   God **forgive** you!   Heaven **help** us!
   Heaven **forbid** that you should think that of me.
   Suffice it to say he escaped with only a caution.

2 I only ask that he **cease** to follow this line of
   questioning.
   It is vital that they **be** stopped at once.
   Is it really necessary that she **work** all hours of the day?
   I demand that he **do** something to make up for this.

3 I only ask that **he should cease** to follow this line of
   questioning.
   It is vital that they **are** stopped at once.
   It is vital **to stop** them at once.
   Is it really necessary **for her to work** all hours of the
   day?
   I demand that **he does** something to make up for this.

4 If your father **were** alive he would help you.
   If I **were** rich I would buy a Mercedes.
   I wish I **were** really rich.
   If only he **were** here now!

5 You talk as if he **were** your owner!
   Some people behave as though dogs **were** human.

6 If your father **was** alive he would help you.
   If I **was** rich I would buy a Mercedes.
   I wish I **was** really rich.
   If only he **was** here now!
   You talk as if he **was** your owner!

Exclamations

Exclamations are short utterances that a speaker makes when very surprised or upset. They are not always whole sentences. Sometimes they are more like a noise than a word. In this case they are called **interjections** ($\rightarrow$ 1). Many exclamations consist of just one word ($\rightarrow$ 2).

Exclamations can also consist of:
    what + **noun phrase** ($\rightarrow$ 3) or *how* + **adjective** ($\rightarrow$ 4).
They may also have the form of a negative question ($\rightarrow$ 5).

- Another form of exclamation is when the hearer repeats part of the sentence that he or she has just heard. This is used when the hearer finds it hard to believe what has been said or is very surprised. This sort of exclamation is called an **echo** ($\rightarrow$ 6).

Responses

Responses are made in answer to a question or a statement by another person in the course of conversation. Like exclamations, they may be full sentences, but can also be phrases or single words ($\rightarrow$ 7). Responses usually do not make sense on their own.

Although a response may not have a subject or contain a main verb, it can be classed as a sentence, because a response uses our knowledge of what has just been said. The subject or the verb will usually be understood from the context ($\rightarrow$ 8).

- If the verb is in a simple tense you can use the supporting auxiliary *do* as the verb in the response ($\rightarrow$ 9).
- You usually just use the first part of the verb phrase in a compound verb to make a response. That is, one of the **auxiliary** verbs ($\rightarrow$ 10) or a **modal verb** becomes the response form ($\rightarrow$ 11). Some speakers prefer to use the modal and the auxiliary form together ($\rightarrow$ 12).

1 Ugh!   Phew!
  Wow!   Huh!

2 Help!   Nonsense!
  Blast!   Rubbish!

3 **What** a pity!   **What** a lovely day!
  What rubbish!

4 **How** silly !   **How** kind of him!

5 **Isn't** it a warm day!   **Aren't** they kind!

6 Geoff's passed the exam with an A grade. – **Geoff's passed the exam!**
  Sally's engaged. – **She's engaged!** How exciting!

7 Yes.
  On Tuesday.
  I certainly will.

8 Are you coming to the party tonight? – **Yes**.
  When are you going to London, then? – **On Tuesday**.
  Will you be doing some shopping? – **I certainly will**.

9 Do you like courgettes? – Yes, I **do**.

10 Has Tammy called round yet? – Yes, she **has**.
   Was that Andrea? – Yes, it **was**.

11 May we leave early? – Yes, you **may**.
   Should I turn it on? – No, you **shouldn't**.

12 Laurence could be running if it wasn't for his injury. – Yes, he **could be**.

Sentences and Clauses

A clause is a group of words which contains a verb.
The verb in a clause can be finite (→ 1) or non-finite (→ 2).

Simple sentences
Simple sentences consist of one clause, in which the verb
is finite (→ 3). Two or more clauses can be joined to make
a **compound** sentence or a **complex** sentence.

Complex sentences
Complex sentences are those that contain a **subordinate**
clause as well as a **main** clause (→ 4). A **subordinate**
clause is one that contains special information about the
main clause. It will usually be introduced by a **linking**
word such as *when, if, because,* or *that*. The linking words
are called **subordinating conjunctions.**

Most subordinate clauses can come before, after, or within
the main clause. Usually, when one clause is of principal
importance and the other clause gives information about the
principal one, we have a complex sentence with one **main**
clause and one **subordinate clause**.

- The position that a subordinate clause is placed in is
  determined largely by what is felt to be the main
  message of a sentence (→ 5).

Compound sentences
A compound sentence is one that consists of two **main**
clauses, joined by a word such as *and, but, or,* called a
coordinating conjunction. Each clause is of equal
importance and gives information of equal value.
The order of the clauses can be very important for the
meaning. For example, the timing of an action can be
described by the order in which the clauses follow each
other (→ 6).

Compound-complex sentences
These have more than one main clause and at least one
subordinate clause (→ 7).

1 **Use** water only.
  He **missed** the turnoff.

2 **To clean**, use water only.
  Dreaming about Jenny, he missed the turnoff.

3 Ann **went** to the bank.
  She **withdrew** £100.

4 *When he arrives,* **I'll phone you.**
  He stayed at home *because he felt ill*.

5 **Since you seem to have made up your mind**, I'll
  say no more.
  I stopped seeing her **because she was engaged to
  Philip**.

6 He picked it up **and** ran over to her.
  He ran over to her **and** picked it up.
  I drove to Coatbridge **and** went on to Stirling **and
  then** I drove to Berwick.
  I drove to Stirling **and then** I went to Coatbridge.

7 I met Angie **and** we decided to use my car **because**
  hers was unreliable.
  He ran over to Julie, **who** was sitting at the end of the
  bench, **and** snatched up her handbag.

Joining Clauses

Coordination

The process called **coordination** joins two short clauses of
equal importance with a conjunction. Each clause becomes
a **main** clause in the new sentence (→ 1).

The clauses are linked by words called **coordinating
conjunctions**, such as *and, but, (either) or, neither, nor,
yet*. Conjunctions come right at the beginning of a clause.

● If the subject of both clauses is the same, it does not
  have to be repeated in front of the second verb.

The conjunction *and* is used:
− to join clauses where there is no contrast or choice.
− to join more than two clauses; the earlier clauses can be
  joined by a comma, but the last two must be joined
  by *and* (→ 2).

The conjunction *but* is used to join clauses where there is
a contrast (→ 3).

The conjunction *yet* is used to join clauses where there is a
contrast that is of a somewhat surprising nature (→ 4).

● The conjunctions *and, but, or, neither*, and *nor* are also
  used to join two phrases of the same kind (→ 5), or two
  words of the same class (→ 6). In particular, *and* and
  but are used to coordinate pairs of adjectives in a
  predicative position (→ 6).

Continued

1 Ann went to the bank **and** withdrew £100.
   Sally goes to work **but** Ann doesn't have a job.
   Ann (**either**) stays at home **or** visits her family.

2 Ann got into the car, drove to the bank, withdrew £100,
   and went shopping for a coat.

3 She planned to buy a new dress **but** she couldn't find a
   nice one.

4 Susan always gets up early, **yet** Jane, who never gets
   up before nine, always gets to work earlier.
   He loved her **yet** he couldn't bring himself to propose.

5 This device is useful for **matching colours and
   touching them up**.
   The former President and his wife were there.

6 I use this chair when I am **reading and working.**
   Do you undertake **detailed or intricate** work?
   Jack and Jill fell down the hill.
   a **complicated but intriguing** task

7 *Compare:*
   He is a **tall, merry** person with a shock of white hair.
   He is **tall and merry**, with a shock of white hair.
   She seemed scared **but** elated at the same time.

Coordination (ctd)

When there is a positive choice between the subjects of two clauses, you use the pair of words *either* and *or* to join the clauses (→ 1). If the subject of the joined clauses is the same, the subject is used in the first of the joined clauses only. This is often also true of any auxiliary verbs that may be present (→ 2).

When it is used in this way *either* must come in one of these places:
- before the subject in the first clause of the group.
- in front of the main verb and after any auxiliary verb. You can use *either...or* to join more than two clauses if you repeat the use of *or* (→ 3).The use of *either...or* emphasizes that the two clauses are alternatives and cannot both be true. Compare *and...or* (→ 4).

The word *either* can be left out if the sentence meaning is clear. Some writers treat all but the final *or* as optional.

• You can use *or* on its own to join two or more clauses, but *either* cannot be used on its own.

When there is a negative choice between the subjects of two clauses, you can use the pair of words *neither* and *nor* to join the clauses (→ 5).

The word *neither* can be used on its own to connect two clauses if the first clause contains a word with broad negative meaning such as *not*, *barely* or *scarcely* (→ 6). The word *nor* can also be used like this. If you use *neither* or *nor* in this way, and if there is a subject in the second clause, question order must be used (→ 5), (→ 6).

• The words *either* and *neither* can also be used as a pronoun or as a determiner. Each can then be used on its own; it does not then have a joining function (→ 7).

• *either, or, neither,* and *nor* can be used as conjunctions inside a noun phrase or a verb phrase (→ 8).

1 **Either** you come to my place **or** I'll meet you at work,
   which do you prefer?

2 Martin said he would **either** meet them for lunch **or**
   take them to tea.

3 Colin said he would (**either**) meet them for lunch, (**or**)
   take them to tea, **or** see them next week.
   Ian can (**either**) come with us **or** take a taxi later.

4 Colin said he would meet them for lunch, take them to
   tea, **and / or** see them next week.

5 Rochelle **neither** wants to come with us **nor** be left on
   her own.
   Jane was **not** a fool, **neither / nor was she** prepared
   to be made the scapegoat.

6 There was **scarcely** enough meat for the children, **neither did they** have any bread.
   Eric **hardly** saw the fight, **nor did he** remember
   much about the incident later.

7 **Either** book will do. It doesn't matter.
   Neither book is at all suitable, I'm sorry.
   You can have **either**.

8 You can choose to study **either** *Shakespeare* **or**
   Keats.
   Neither *Vimala* **nor** *Katie* knew the answer.
   She is **either** *desperate* **or** *just silly*.
   He didn't know whether *to come* **or** *go*.

Subordination

When two or more clauses are joined by a conjunction other than *and*, *but*, *or*, or *yet*, one of the clauses is the main clause; the other clauses are **subordinate** clauses. The different types of subordinate clause include **noun** clauses (→ 1), **adverbial** clauses (→ 2), **relative** clauses (→ 3), **conditional** clauses (→ 4), and **reported** clauses (→ 5).

Each of the subordinate clauses is associated with an introductory word that signals what type of clause it is that follows (→ 6). These words are called **subordinating conjunctions**. They include:
– the **WH-** words
– words like *since, if, when, because*
– the word *that*, either on its own or used with another word e.g. *so that* or *supposing that*
– a phrase ending in *as*, e.g. *as soon as, as long as*

• Each of the subordinating clauses has a preferred position. For example, most adverbial clauses usually follow the main clause, although they can also come before the main clause or divide the main clause (→ 7). Reported clauses usually follow directly on from the main reporting clause. See p. 246.

Noun Clauses

These are clauses that can be used as either the subject or the object of a sentence or in other places where a noun phrase is usually found. They are introduced by *that* (→ 8) or by a **WH-** word, e.g. *who, when, where* (→ 9). Word order after a **WH-** word is the same as in a statement.

• The subordinating conjunction *that* can often be omitted (→ 10).

1 What matters most is **that you give us a fair hearing**.

2 They went outside **as soon as the shooting stopped**.

3 The tiles, **which had been rattling violently**, started to fly off.

4 Maureen plans to live in Australia **if she can get a job there.**

5 She told me **that Philip was in France**.

6 **After** she had read the diary, she returned it to the drawer.
As they were going downstairs, the phone rang.
He isn't coming with us **because** they quarrelled.

7 Shall I do the shopping **when I finish work**?
When I finish work, I could do the shopping for you.
Harry had found, **when he was living in Jamaica,**
several old silver coins.

8 **That he will succeed** is very probable.

9 I don't know **where you live**.
How the thief got in is a mystery.
Why she acts like this is beyond me.

10 It is very probable **that he will succeed**.
It is very probable **he will succeed**.

Adverbial clauses

Adverbial clauses generally follow the main clause unless otherwise stated. The following are the main types of adverbial clause.

Time: sets the timing for the main clause (→ 1).
– may come before or after the main clause.
– introduced by *after, as, as soon as, before, once, since, till, the moment (that), until, whenever, when, while.*

Place: sets where the action of the main clause takes place (→ 2).
– introduced by *where, wherever,* or *everywhere.*

Manner: sets out how the main clause was carried out.
– introduced by *as, as if, as though, how, just as,* or *the way that* (→ 3).

Reason: sets out the thinking behind the action of the main clause (→ 4).
– may come before or after the main clause.
– introduced by *as, because,* or *since.*

Purpose: sets out what it was hoped would be achieved by carrying out the action of the main clause (→ 5).
– introduced by *so that, in order that, in case,* or *lest.*
• Purpose can also be indicated by *so as to, in order to* followed by the base form of a verb (→ 6).

Result: sets out what happened when the main clause was carried out (→ 7).
– introduced by **so + adjective / adverb** + *that* or by **such a + noun phrase** + *that.*

Contrast: suggests that something else may need to be taken into account regarding the main clause (→ 8).
– may come before or after the main clause.
– introduced by *although, even though, even if, however, much as,* or *while.*

1 We should go **as soon as you are ready**.
   I'll call for you **whenever you like**.
   Since my father died, I have not been able to sleep.
   We shall leave **the moment (that) you want to**.

2 Put it **where you want**.
   She went **everywhere that she wanted**.
   Wherever you looked, he was to be found.

3 Mandy looked **as if she had seen a ghost**.
   Earl wandered in, **the way that he does**.
   You have to fasten it **as though it was a shoelace**.
   The room was prepared **just as he had requested**.
   Just do it **how I ask you**.

4 I don't want to go **because I can't stand old Chaplin
   movies**.
   I thought you would be ready **since you were calling
   me**.

5 Put it just there **so that it holds the door open**.
   Leave a little for Becky **in case she wants some
   supper**.

6 He put it down **so as to hold the door open**.
   He put it against the door **in order to hold it open**.

7 Ben was **so** angry **that he kicked the wall hard**.
   That cat is **so** beautiful **that I can't keep my eyes off
   her**.
   Gloria is **such** a generous person **that she is often
   short of money**.

8 **However much you may want to spend your sav-
   ings**, try to keep something in reserve.
   Although it has rained, the ground is still very dry.
   We must try to do something for the starving and
   homeless, **even if we can't solve all the world's
   problems**.

Relative Clauses

Relative clauses tell us more about nouns. They function rather like adjectives and are found as **postmodifiers** in a noun phrase. The noun that is modified is called the **antecedent**. Relative clauses normally begin with *who, whom, whose,* or *that*.

These words are called **relative pronouns**. Note that some of them also function as interrogative pronouns. See also p. 188.
A relative pronoun can be the subject ($\rightarrow$ 1) or object ($\rightarrow$ 2) of the verb in the relative clause. If it is the object it can be left out in ordinary informal speech and writing ($\rightarrow$ 3). Subject and object relative pronouns come at the beginning of the relative clause.

- A relative pronoun can also be the object of a preposition ($\rightarrow$ 4). In informal English a relative clause can end in a preposition, especially if the relative pronoun is omitted ($\rightarrow$ 5).

Defining and non-defining relative clauses
There are two sorts of relative clause.
Some relative clauses act rather like an adjective by providing more information about a particular noun ($\rightarrow$ 6). These are called **defining** relative clauses or **restrictive** relative clauses. This type of clause is used to limit the possible reference of a noun to what the clause tells us about it ($\rightarrow$ 7).

A defining relative clause is never separated from the noun by a comma. It is also often marked by using the relative pronoun *that* or by using no relative pronoun at all ($\rightarrow$ 3), ($\rightarrow$ 6).

The other type of relative clause adds extra information to the whole of the main clause. These are **non-defining relative clauses** or **non-restrictive** relative clauses. This type of clause is separated from the main clause by commas ($\rightarrow$ 8).

1   The people **who live upstairs** are having a party.
     People shouldn't have parties **that last all night**.

2   I don't like the music **that they are playing**.
     A man **whom I met on the stairs** said it was an all-
     night party.

3   I don't like the music **they are playing**.
     A man **I met on the stairs** said it was an all-night
     party.

4   The man **to whom I sold my car** was a musician.
     This marvellous game, **at which we can all excel** if
     we want, is called croquet.

5   The man **I sold my car to** was a musician.
     This marvellous game, **which we can all excel at** if
     we want, is called croquet.

6   The people **who / that live upstairs** are having a
     party.
     I don't like the music **that they are playing**.
     The girl **who was on the bus with us** is called Sonia.

7   *Defining.*
     The brother **who / that lives in Canada** is a lawyer.
     There are several brothers. The Canadian one is a lawyer.

     Non-defining.
     The brother, **who lives in Canada**, is a lawyer.
     *There is only one brother. He is a lawyer. He happens to
     live in Canada.*

8   The man upstairs, **by whom I mean my lodger**, is a
     very quiet person.
     Fred went off alone, **which was a real blessing**.
     At least tennis gives you some strenuous exercise,
     which is a good reason for taking up the sport.

Conditional Clauses

Conditional sentences consist of a main clause and a
conditional clause (sometimes called an *if*-clause).
The conditional clause usually begins with *if* or *unless*.
The conditional clause can come before or after the main
clause (→ 1). There are three main types of conditional
sentence.

Type 1

The main clause uses *will, can, may,* or *might* + the
base form of a main verb. The *if*-clause uses the Simple
Present tense (→ 2).
Type 1 sentences refer to the future. They suggest that the
action in the main clause is quite likely to happen (→ 3).
The use of the modal verb *may* or *might* in the main clause
suggests that there is some doubt whether the main verb
action will be achieved (→ 4).

Type 2

The main clause uses *would, could,* or *might* + the **base
form** of a main verb. The *if*-clause uses the Simple Past
tense (→ 5) or the past subjunctive (→ 7).
Type 2 sentences refer to an imaginary situation. They
imply that the action in the *if*-clause will probably not
happen (→ 6). They are often used when giving advice to
someone, especially about what the person should do (→ 7).

Type 3

The main clause uses *would, could,* or *might* + *have* +
the **past participle** of a main verb. The *if*-clause uses
the Past Perfect tense (→ 8).
In Type 3 sentences the speaker is looking back from the
present to a past time and event. The speaker is talking
about what might have happened but did not, either
because the wrong thing was done or because nothing was
done. This type of sentence is used when making excuses
and recriminations or giving an explanation.

Continued

1 We'll be late **if we don't leave now**.
   We'll be late **unless we leave now**.
   If we don't leave now, we'll be late.
   Unless we leave now, we'll be late.

2 **If you take the first bus**, you will be in time.
   She'll be cold **if she doesn't wear a coat**.
   If you want more helpers, I can come.

3 They **will** not finish their homework unless they start
   now.
   If you book early, you **will** get a seat.

4 If you book early, you **may** get a seat.
   Mary **might** deliver your parcel, if you ask her.

5 If Jim **lent** us his car, we could go to the picnic.
   We would save £1.50 a day if we **didn't eat** any lunch.
   If a burglar **broke** into my house, he would not find
   any money.
   Would you be very angry if I **failed** my exam?

6 If I won the pools, I would buy a big house.
   (But I do not think I will win the pools.)
   If you didn't spend all your money on cigarettes, you
   could afford a holiday.
   (But you do spend all your money on cigarettes.)

7 **If I were you**, I'd marry her straight away.

8 We could have taken a longer holiday, if we **had not
   spent** so much money on the garden this year.
   If I **had known** before today that he wasn't serious, I
   might have wasted less time on the project.

Conditional Clauses (ctd)

Conditional clauses can also be used to talk about
consequences or to give an opinion about a situation in the
following ways:

– the *if*-clause uses the Simple Present tense and the
  main clause uses the Simple Present tense.
  This is used to refer to universal truths (→ 1).

– the *if*-clause uses the Simple Present tense and the
  main clause is in the imperative mood.
  This is used to give advice or orders for particular
  situations or sets of circumstances (→ 2).

– the *if*-clause uses the Present Progressive or Simple
  Present tense and the main clause uses a modal verb.
  This is used to make suggestions and give advice (→ 3).

– the *if*-clause uses *will / would* and the main clause
  uses a modal verb.
  This is used to make a request or give a polite order (→ 4).

• Note that a *'d* in the main clause is the contracted form
  of *would*. However, a *'d* in an if-clause is the contracted
  form of *had* (→ 5).

In the main clause the contracted forms of the modals
used in speech and informal writing are:

I'd have *or*	**I would've**
I could've	**I might've**

1 If you **heat** water to 100°C, it **boils**.
   Plants **die** if they **don't get** enough water.

2 If you **want** an appointment, **phone** in advance.
   If a red light **shows** here, **switch off** the machine.

3 If you **are thinking of** buying a lawnmower, you **can**
   try my new one first.
   He **should** turn down his radio if he **doesn't want** to
   get into trouble.

4 If **you'll** wait a minute, the doctor **can** see you.
   If you **would** sign here, please, **I'll** be able to send you
   the books.

5 **I'd** have gone if **he'd** invited me.
   I **would** have gone **if he had invited me**.
   I **would've** gone if **he'd** invited me.

Reporting Speech

There are two ways of writing down or reporting what was said on any occasion. We can repeat the actual words used (**direct speech**) ($\rightarrow$ 1), or we can build the words into our own sentences (**reported speech**) ($\rightarrow$ 2). The words reported are normally accompanied by a **reporting verb** ($\rightarrow$ 3). Another name for reported speech is **indirect speech**.

Direct Speech

Direct speech gives the actual words that the speaker used. It is common in novels and other writing where the actual words of a speaker are quoted ($\rightarrow$ 1).

The **reporting verb** may come before the words that were actually spoken, or after them, or at a natural pause inside the reported sentence ($\rightarrow$ 4).

- Typical reporting verbs are: *agree, answer, ask, inquire, explain, say, tell,* and *wonder.*

The subject and the reporting verb are sometimes reversed ($\rightarrow$ 5).

The actual words spoken always begin with a capital letter, unless the reporting verb comes within a sentence. They are separated from the reporting verb by a comma, unless they are followed by a question mark or an exclamation ($\rightarrow$ 6).

- The words spoken are enclosed in inverted commas ('single' or "double" quotation marks). Double quotation marks are more common, especially in handwriting ($\rightarrow$ 7), but single quotation marks may be used instead ($\rightarrow$ 8). Either may be used.

- Single quotation marks are often used to draw attention to a word that is being mentioned for a particular purpose ($\rightarrow$ 9).

1   Monica said, **"There is a new film on at the Odeon."**

2   Monica said that there was a new film on at the Odeon.

3   Monica **said / declared** that there was a new film at the Odeon.
    "There is a new film on at the Odeon," Monica **replied**.

4   **Monica said,** "There is a new film on at the Odeon."
    "There is a new film on at the Odeon," **Monica said.**
    "There is," **Monica said,** "a new film on at the Odeon."

5   "There is a new film on at the Odeon," **said Monica.**

6   "Why did you do it?" she shouted.
    "Oh, mind your own business!" he snapped back.

7   **"I've already seen it,"** John replied.

8   **'Have you been to the new shopping precinct yet?'** asked Shona.
    'No,' said Philippa, **'but I hear that it has some really nice shops.'**

9   There is no such word as 'fubber'.
    He called me a 'yodelling nincompoop'!

Reported Speech

Reported speech or **indirect speech** reports something that was said, but does not use the actual words that the speaker uttered ($\rightarrow$ 1).

Reported speech always has two clauses. The words spoken are put in a **reported clause**. There is also a **main clause** that contains a **reporting verb**. The main clause with the reporting verb usually comes before the **reported clause** ($\rightarrow$ 2).

The reporting verb in the main clause tells us how the sentence was uttered, e.g. *comment, remark, say, tell*.
If the reported clause is a **statement**, the main clause is linked to the reported clause by *that* ($\rightarrow$ 3).
If the reported clause asks a question, the main verb will be a question verb e.g. *ask, inquire, wonder, query*. The link between the main clause and the reported clause will be *if* or *whether* ($\rightarrow$ 4).

- The linking word *that* can be left out after most reporting verbs, but the links *if* or *whether* cannot be left out ($\rightarrow$ 5).

- Speech in a reported clause is not separated from the reporting verb by a comma, is not enclosed in inverted commas, and does not begin with a capital letter unless it is a proper noun. Reported questions are not followed by question marks.

An alternative position for main clauses that would normally have a linking *that*, is after the reported clause ($\rightarrow$ 6). In this case, the link is left out.

- Reported clauses can also be used to express what is in someone's mind as well as what is actually spoken ($\rightarrow$ 7).

Continued

1 **Shona asked** whether Philippa had been to the new shopping precinct. **Philippa replied** that she had not, but **she had heard** that it had some really nice shops.

2 **The newspaper says** that the Prime Minister is going to resign.
   Peter enquired if Mandy was feeling better.

3 Mary said **that** her favourite actor was Robert Redford. John replied **that** he preferred Greta Scacchi.

4 Miriam asked **if** she could borrow Leonie's new records. Evelyn wondered **whether** the concert would be sold out.

5 Victor told Nicholas (**that**) he had passed his driving test.
   Lucy heard Alan had been accepted to do VSO.

6 *Batman* was on that night**, Mary said**.

7 Evelyn **wondered** whether **the concert would be sold out**.
   Charlene **thought** that **she had better go and see her family**.

Reported Speech (ctd)

Changes in the reported words

When you use reported speech, the words put into the reported clause do not exactly match the words actually spoken ($\to$ 1).

Pronouns and **possessive determiners** have to change in reported speech because of the change of speaker, e.g. *I* may become *she*; *you* may become *us* or *him* ($\to$ 2). Expressions of place and time may also have to change, e.g. *here* may become *there* or *home*; *Friday* may become *in three days' time* ($\to$ 3).

The tense in reported clauses

The verb in the direct speech may also change, e.g. *must* becomes *had to* in reported speech. The most common change is a change of tense ($\to$ 5).

A reporting verb in the present tense can be used in the main clause when you report on a letter or on a recent conversation, e.g. a telephone conversation ($\to$ 4). However, it is more common to use a past tense when reporting speech. In this case, the verb in direct speech changes to a past tense when it becomes part of reported speech ($\to$ 5).

The changes of tense may be summarized as follows:

Direct speech	Reported speech
Simple Present	Simple Past
Present Progressive	Past Progressive
Present Perfect	Past Perfect
Present Perfect Progressive	Past Perfect Progressive
Simple Past	Past Perfect or Simple Past
Future	Conditional

Continued

1 *"I'll leave here at 8.30 on Friday."*
   She says **that she will leave home at 8.30 tomorrow**.

   "I'm looking forward to seeing you."
   She says **she's looking forward to seeing us**.

2 *"I believe you."*
   She said that **she** believed **us**.

   "I am leaving you."
   She said that **she** was leaving **him**.

   "I have finished."
   She said that **she had finished**.

3 *"I have been here before."*
   She said that she **had been there already**.

   "I will see you on Monday."
   She said that she would see him **in three days' time**.

4 *"Hello, Jake? I've arrived here on time and I'll take a bus to your place."*
   Penny has just phoned. She **says** that she has arrived on time and that **she's taking** a bus here.

5 *"Hello Jake? It's me, Penny. I've arrived here on time and I'll take a bus to your place. One is coming now, so I must run."*

   She rang to say that **she had** arrived **at New Street Station** on time and **would** take a bus to **our** place. She went on to say that one **was** coming **at that very moment**, so **she had to** run.

   "I've bought my ticket."
   Sally says **she has bought her ticket**.

Reported Speech (ctd)

Questions

Verb tenses in reported questions undergo the same
changes as in statements ($\rightarrow$ 1), ($\rightarrow$ 2). See p. 248.

- Reporting verbs for questions include *ask, inquire, want
  to know*, and *wonder*.

Direct **polar** questions *(yes / no)* are linked to the
reporting clause by *if* or **whether**. **WH–** question words,
e.g. *who, when, where*, are used in both direct and indirect
questions ($\rightarrow$ 1), ($\rightarrow$ 2).

- The word order in a reported question is the same as
  that of a direct statement. Question order is not used in
  reported speech, i.e. no part of the verb comes before the
  subject.

Orders and requests

Orders are reported with *tell* + **object** + *to infinitive* ($\rightarrow$ 3).

Requests for action are reported with *ask* + **object** + *to
infinitive* ($\rightarrow$ 4).

Requests for objects are reported with *ask for* + **object** ($\rightarrow$ 5).

- The reporting verb can be used in the passive ($\rightarrow$ 6).

Suggestions, advice, promises, etc.

A variety of verbs can be used for reporting suggestions
and similar types of speech. Some of these are:
- *suggest, insist on* + Present participle ($\rightarrow$ 7)
- *advise, invite, warn* + direct object + *not* + *to* infinitive ($\rightarrow$ 8)
- *refuse, threaten* + *to* infinitive ($\rightarrow$ 9)
- *offer, promise* + *to* infinitive ($\rightarrow$ 10)

1 *"Are you ready?"*
He asked (us) if / whether we **were** ready.

2 *"What time is it?"*
He inquired what time it **was**.
"Where has Jim gone?"
He wanted to know where Jim **had gone**.

3 *"Stop smoking!"*
"You must stop smoking."
The doctor **told him to stop** smoking.

4 *"Please don't smoke in the kitchen."*
She asked us **not to smoke** in the kitchen.

5 *"May I have the salt?"*
He **asked for the salt**.

6 *"Don't park here!"*
I was **told not to park** there.

7 *"Let's go to the zoo."*
He suggested going to the zoo.

8 *"I wouldn't buy that one, if I were you."*
She advised me **not to buy** that one.

9 *"I certainly won't tell you!"*
She **refused to tell** me.

10 *"I'll help you."*
He **promised to help** me.

INDEX